3 All-Star
Student Workbook

Linda Lee

Kristin Sherman ★ Grace Tanaka ★ Shirley Velasco

Second Edition

McGraw Hill

Connect
Learn
Succeed™

ALL-STAR 3: WORKBOOK

3 4 5 6 7 8 9 0 QVR/QVR 1 0 9 8 7 6 5 4 3

Workbook

ISBN 978-0-07-719723-0
MHID 0-07-719723-2

ISE

ISBN 978-0-07-131388-9
MHID 0-07-131388-5

Vice president/Editor in chief: *Elizabeth Haefele*
Vice president/Director of marketing: *John E. Biernat*
Director of development, ESL Domestic: *Valerie E. Kelemen*
Developmental editor: *Laura LeDrean*
Director of sales and marketing, ESL Domestic: *Pierre Montagano*
Lead digital product manager: *Damian Moshak*
Digital developmental editor: *Kevin White*
Director, Editing/Design/Production: *Jess Ann Kosic*
Project manager: *Jean R. Starr*
Senior production supervisor: *Debra R. Sylvester*
Senior designer: *Srdjan Savanovic*
Senior photo research coordinator: *Lori Kramer*
Photo researcher: *Allison Grimes*
Digital production coordinator: *Brent dela Cruz*
Typeface: *11/13 Frutiger Roman*
Compositor: *Laserwords Private Limited*
Printer: *Quad/Graphics*
Cover credit: *Andrew Lange*
Credits: The credits section for this book begins on page 185 and is considered an extension of the copyright page.

All-Star is a four-level, standards-based series for English learners featuring a picture-dictionary approach to vocabulary building. "Big picture" scenes in each unit provide springboards to a wealth of activities developing all of the language skills. Each *All-Star* Workbook unit provides 18 pages of supplementary activities for its corresponding Student Book unit. The workbook activities offer students further practice in developing the language, vocabulary, and life-skill competencies taught in the Student Book. Answers to the Workbook activities are available in the Teacher's Edition.

Workbook Features

★ **Standards coverage complements the Student Book** for a comprehensive program covering all revised national standards: CASAS, SCANS, EFF, Florida, LAUSD, Texas, and others.

★ **Wide range of exercises** can be used by students working independently or in groups, in the classroom, with a tutor, or at home. Each unit includes several activities that allow students to interact, usually by asking and answering questions.

★ **Alternate application lessons** complement the Student Book application lesson, inviting students to tackle work, family, and/or community extension activities in each unit.

★ **Student Book page references** at the top of each Workbook page show how the two components support one another.

★ **Practice tests** at the end of each unit provide practice answering multiple-choice questions such as those found on the CASAS tests. Students are invited to chart their progress on these tests on a bar graph on the inside back cover.

★ **Crossword puzzles and word searches** reinforce unit vocabulary.

Alternate Application Lessons (Work, Family, Community)

Equipped for the Future (EFF) is a set of standards for adult literacy and lifelong learning developed by The National Institute for Literacy (www.nifl.gov). The organizing principle of EFF is that adults assume responsibilities in three major areas of life—as workers, as parents, and as citizens. These three areas of focus are called "role maps" in the EFF documentation.

Lesson 4 in each unit of the Student Book provides a real-life application relating to one of the learners' roles. The Workbook includes two alternate application lessons that expand on two of the three roles. This allows you, as the teacher, to customize the unit to meet the needs of your students. You can teach any or all of the application lessons in class. For example, if all your students work, you may choose to focus on the work applications. If your students have diverse interests and needs, you may have them work in small groups on different applications. If your program provides many hours of classroom time each week, you have the material to cover all three roles.

Contents

Identifying Responsibilities

A Complete the paragraph below using the simple present form of the verbs in the box. You may use a verb more than once. Some of the answers are negative.

be	cook	do	go	have	help	put
spend	shop	plan	take	wash	want	work

Laura and Ed Martin (1) _____ always busy. Laura (2) _____ full-time at a hotel, and Ed (3) _____ an electrician. They (4) _____ two children, Michael and Jennifer. They (5) _____ to buy a new house, so they (6) _____ a lot of money. The children (7) _____ to school. Laura (8) _____ classes at the community college. She (9) _____ to get a job in hotel management. Both Laura and Ed (10) _____ housework. Ed usually (11) _____ grocery shopping and (12) _____ away the groceries. Laura usually (13) _____ the meals. Michael often (14) _____ the dishes. Laura and Ed (15) _____ to PTA meetings. They also (16) _____ their children with homework. Laura and Ed (17) _____ much free time!

B Look at the photo below. What does this family do every morning? Complete the sentences with your own ideas.

1. The mother _____

_____.

2. The father _____

_____.

3. The daughter _____

_____.

C Look at the pie graph. It shows how Laura spends her time on a typical day. Answer the questions.

1. How many hours does Laura study each day? _____

2. How many hours does she sleep? _____

3. How many hours does Laura clean the house? _____

4. How many hours does she work each day? _____

5. How many hours is Laura in class? _____

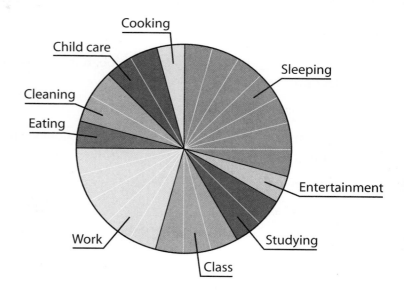

**Daily Activity Graph
(in 1 hour increments)**

Cooking

Child care

Sleeping

Cleaning

Eating

Entertainment

Work

Studying

Class

D Read the questions about a typical day. Answer them with your own information. Write sentences.

1. How many hours do you sleep every night?

_____

2. How many hours do you study every day?

_____

3. How many hours do you take care of children every day?

_____

4. How many hours do you read, or watch TV or movies?

_____

5. How many hours do you commute?

_____

6. How many hours are you in class every day?

_____

7. How many hours do you cook and clean?

_____

8. How many hours do you email, text, or talk on the phone?

_____

Long and Short-Term Goals

A Use the correct forms of the verbs to complete the sentences.

1. would like / need

   Samantha ____would like____ to get a job, but she has a young daughter. She ____needs____ to find daycare.

2. want / need

   Mohammad _____ to check books out of the library. He _____ to get a library card.

3. want / need

   Luz and Paulo _____ to become U.S. citizens. They study, but it is difficult for them. They _____ to find a tutor.

4. want / need

   I _____ to pay off my debts, so I _____ to save money.

5. would like / need

   I _____ to study every day, but I am very busy with my part-time job, my family, and my friends. I _____ to prioritize.

6. would like / need

   Monica _____ to take academic classes, but she doesn't know what she wants to study. She _____ to see an academic counselor.

B Cross out the word that has a different meaning.

1. reduce   cut back   ~~add~~
2. pay off   increase debt   charge
3. tutor   teacher   student
4. prepare   start   get ready
5. payment   financial aid   loan
6. PTA   school meeting practice
7. prioritize   set goals   volunteer

C What do Boris and Noriko want to do? Read their goals. What do they need to do? Use the ideas in the box, and write sentences.

Boris' Goals:
become a certified nursing assistant
get an evening job
find a girlfriend

Noriko's Goals:
buy a car
do better in her math class
get in shape

exercise	pass a test	read newspaper employment ads
save money	get a tutor	ask a sister for help

1. _Boris wants to become a certified nursing assistant. He needs to pass a test._
2. _____
3. _____
4. _____
5. _____
6. _____

D Write the correct word form on the line.

Noun	Verb
application	apply
priority	_____
reduction	_____
_____	pay
_____	volunteer
preparation	_____

Identifying Steps to Achieve Goals

A Read the conversation.

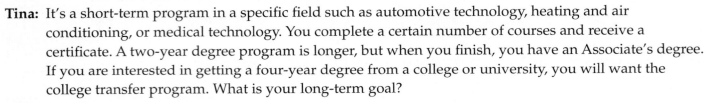

Paul: Hi. I'm Paul Madison. I have an appointment with Tina Walker.

Tina: I'm Tina Walker. Please sit down. How can I help you today?

Paul: I'm planning on taking classes here at the community college in the fall, and I wanted to figure out which classes I should register for.

Tina: Okay. Did you finish high school?

Paul: No, but I got my GED.

Tina: Good. So you don't need adult high school or GED classes. Are you interested in a vocational certificate program, a two-year degree, or the college transfer program?

Paul: I'm not sure. What is a vocational certificate program?

Tina: It's a short-term program in a specific field such as automotive technology, heating and air conditioning, or medical technology. You complete a certain number of courses and receive a certificate. A two-year degree program is longer, but when you finish, you have an Associate's degree. If you are interested in getting a four-year degree from a college or university, you will want the college transfer program. What is your long-term goal?

Paul: I'd like to be an electrician.

Tina: Then you will need the certificate program in electrical/electronics technology. Here is the college catalog. The description of your program is on page 39.

Paul: How long will it take me to finish?

Tina: If you take four courses each term, you will be finished in two terms.

B Answer the questions using complete sentences.

1. What do you think is Tina's job? _____

2. What three kinds of programs are available at the community college?

_____

_____

_____

3. What is Paul's long-term goal? _____

4. What program will Paul take to reach his goal? _____

C Read the information below.

⊠ ⊟ ⊞   LACD

Los Angeles Community College District

| COLLEGE CATALOG | PROSPECTIVE STUDENTS | CURRENT STUDENTS | BUSINESS COMMUNITY |

College Catalog and Programs of Study

Vocational Certificate (18 hours)	Associate in Applied Science (career-oriented program, 72 hours)	General Education (college transfer degree, at least 64 hours)
Automotive Maintenance Culinary Technology—Baking Electrical/Electronics Technology Heating and Air Conditioning Office Systems Technology Restaurant Management Welding	Accounting Computer Programming Culinary Arts Dental Hygiene Early Childhood Associate Electrical/Electronics Engineering Medical Assisting Physical Therapy Assisting	Associate in Arts (English, history, political science) Associate in Science (biology, psychology, engineering, architecture) Associate in Fine Arts (art, music, dance)

D Read about each student's goals. Then, complete the chart.

Student	Program of Study	Area of Study
Miriam wants to be the head chef in a restaurant.	Associate	Culinary Arts
Jerome would like to study engineering at the university.		
Lana is interested in a two-year degree so she can be a physical therapy assistant.		
Rich wants to be a welder.		
Trang wants to work in a day care center.		

Person interviewed	What they want to be doing five years from now	What they will learn or do first to reach their goal

Unit 1: Setting Goals

Becoming a Citizen

A Read the information about the naturalization test. Then number these steps to show the correct order.

_____ a. Have your fingerprints taken.

_____ b. Study for the interview and test.

_____ c. Receive an appointment for an interview.

_____ d. Pass the test and the interview.

_____ e. Go to a USCIS office for your interview.

_____ f. Turn in the Application for Naturalization.

USCIS.GOV

U.S. Citizenship and Immigration Services

HOME   WHAT'S NEW   FAQS   SEARCH   GLOSSARY   FEEDBACK   TRANSLATE   PRINT

About Us

Citizenship Through Naturalization

Citizenship Through Parents

Naturalization Test

Study Materials for the Naturalization Test

Naturalization Self-Test

The Naturalization Test

One of the requirements for U.S. citizenship through naturalization is to take the naturalization test. This test will show that you are able to read, write, and speak basic English and that you have a basic knowledge of U.S. history and government (also known as "civics").

Once you have completed and turned in your Application for Naturalization, you need to have your fingerprints taken at a USCIS office. Then you will receive an appointment for an interview.

English & Civics

During your interview, a USCIS officer will test your ability to read, write, and speak English and your knowledge of civics. You must read one sentence out of three sentences correctly in English, and you must write one sentence out of three sentences correctly in English. The interviewer will evaluate your ability to speak English. Finally, you must answer 6 out of 10 civics questions correctly to pass the test.

You will be given two chances to take the English and civics tests and to answer all questions relating to your naturalization application in English. If you fail any of the tests at your first interview, you will be retested on the test that you failed (English or civics) between 60 and 90 days from the date of your first interview.

Study Materials

We have a variety of study materials to help you learn more about U.S. civics (history and government) as you prepare for the naturalization test. See the "Study Materials for the Naturalization Test" link to the right.

B Answer the questions about the web page in Activity A.

1. What does USCIS stand for?

   _____

2. Why does a person take a naturalization test?

   _____

3. What do you study for the civics test?

   _____

4. Who interviews applicants for naturalization?

   _____

5. Is it necessary to be able to write in English?

   _____

6. How many questions are on the civics test?

   _____

7. How many questions on the civics test must you answer correctly?

   _____

8. If you don't pass the civics test, what can you do?

   _____

9. Where can you find the study materials on the website?

   _____

TAKE IT OUTSIDE: HOW MUCH TO DO YOU KNOW ABOUT U.S. CIVICS? TAKE THE QUIZ BELOW. THEN USE THE INTERNET OR GO TO THE LIBRARY TO CHECK YOUR ANSWERS.

1. Who was the first President? _____

2. Which war did Abraham Lincoln help to end? _____

3. What are the three branches of government? _____

4. When was the Declaration of Independence signed? _____

5. How often do we elect a U.S. Senator? _____

6. Why does the U.S. flag have 50 stars? _____

Reading: Using Context to Guess Meaning

A Read the following article. Underline the important words or phrases that help you guess the meaning of the words in bold.

Keep Your Brain Young

An important goal for many of us is to keep our brains young as we grow old. Usually people experience memory loss and a decrease in **cognitive** ability as their brains get older. But researchers showed that we can slow this process down by keeping our brains **active**. In other words, we need to "use it or lose it."

Crossword puzzles, word games, and other **mental** exercises give our brains the work they need to stay healthy. Taking classes can train our brains to do new things. When our brains focus and solve problems, they exercise.

Research showed that we can improve our memory through physical exercise as well. **Recall** ability increased after six months of regular aerobic exercise, such as running or swimming.

A good diet can also help with cognitive **function**. People who ate green leafy vegetables stayed sharper mentally than people who did not.

B Choose the word with the closest meaning to the words in **bold**. Circle the correct answer.

1. Usually people experience memory loss and a decrease in **cognitive** ability as their brains get older.

   A. physical   B. thinking   C. musical

2. Research shows that we can slow this process down by keeping our brains **active**.

   A. busy   B. quiet   C. slow

3. Taking a class, learning a new language, and doing other **mental** exercises give our brains the work they need to stay healthy.

   A. writing   B. physical   C. thinking

4. People can improve their memory through physical exercise as well. **Recall** ability increased after six months of regular aerobic exercise, such as running or swimming.

   A. memory B. running C. healthy

5. A good diet can also help with cognitive **function**.

   A. food B. exercise C. activity

C Write definitions for the words in **bold**.

1. Many older people have **diminished** brain function, and so have memory loss and other problems in thinking.

   _____

2. When you **concentrate** on solving a problem, you focus your attention on it. This exercises your brain.

   _____

3. Physical **fitness** improves your body's health, of course, but it also aids your mental health.

   _____

4. You increase your **intellectual** activity if you take a class, learn a new skill, or play a difficult game.

   _____

5. People don't have to have a **decline** in their quality of life as they age—they can prevent many of the negative effects of aging by exercising, eating well, and working with their brains.

   _____

6. Jake didn't have enough money to go to college, but with financial aid, he was able to **overcome** this problem.

   _____

7. Susan will get a job because she is **innovative**. She always comes up with new ideas and ways to solve problems.

   _____

8. People who are physically active instead of **sedentary** have a better chance of staying mentally fit.

   _____

Writing: Brainstorming and Making a Cluster Diagram

A Look at the cluster diagram below. Write the ideas in the correct place on the chart.

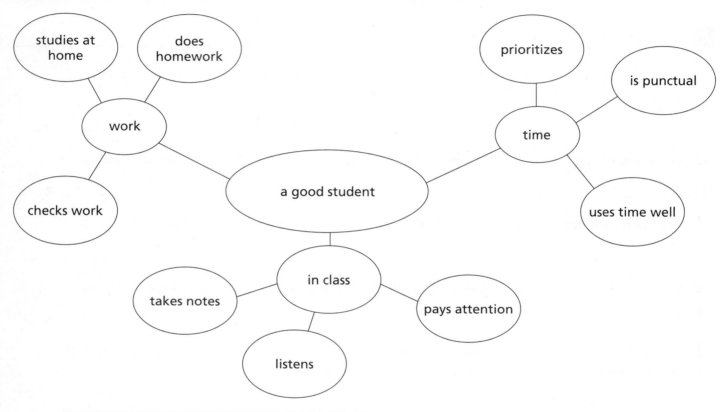

A GOOD STUDENT		
work	**time**	**in class**
studies at home		

B Write three sentences about the qualities of a good student. Use the information in Activity A.

EXAMPLE: *A good student studies at home.*

1. _____

2. _____

3. _____

C Answer the questions.

1. Who was your favorite teacher?

   _____

2. Why did you like him or her?

   _____

3. What kinds of things do you think a good teacher does in class?

   _____

4. How is a good teacher like a good student?

   _____

D Create a cluster diagram in the space below to describe the qualities of a good teacher.

(a good teacher)

E Write three sentences about the qualities of a good teacher.

1. _____

2. _____

3. _____

Family: Talking to Your Child's Teacher

A Read the information.

How to Communicate Better with Your Child's School

One of the most important things you can do to help your child succeed in school is to attend a parent-teacher conference. Just like any important meeting, you can make it a positive experience by following certain steps.

Before the meeting:

1. Schedule an appointment if you need to talk to the teacher. Write a note or make a phone call to set up a convenient time.
2. Gather information. Talk to your child and your spouse and/or other caregivers. Ask what concerns or questions they have.
3. Make a list of what you want to talk about. This will help you remember everything and stay on topic.

During the meeting:

4. Build the relationship. Make small talk. Compliment the teacher if he or she is doing something well.
5. Ask questions about the class and how your child is doing.
6. Deal with problems in a positive way. Ask for specific examples of problems and what seems to help. Develop a plan with the teacher for dealing with the problem in the future. Schedule a time to follow up on the problem. Make sure you know what the teacher will do next.

After the meeting:

7. Talk to your child about the good things he or she is doing and how any problems will be addressed.
8. Follow up with the teacher.

Throughout the year:

9. Stay in touch with the teacher through notes or phone calls.
10. Volunteer at school in the classroom, lunchroom, or library.

B Complete the sentences using information from Activity A.

1. When you want to talk to the teacher, _____ an appointment for a convenient time.

2. If you talk to your child or spouse before the meeting, you can _____ information.

3. Before the meeting, make a _____ of what you want to talk about.

4. _____ the meeting you can ask any questions you would like to ask.

5. Stay in touch with the teacher through _____ or _____.

C Read the statements. In which step of communicating with your child's school do they belong? Write the number of the step from Activity A.

1. "Your teacher said you got an award in math." _____

2. "I'd like to talk to you about Katie's grades. When would be a good time to get together?" _____

3. "Katie is really enjoying your class. She is very excited about school this year." _____

4. "How is Katie's reading?" _____

5. "So in the next week, you will work with Katie on taking notes, and we will monitor how she focuses on homework. Then we'll talk next week." _____

6. "Do you need any help? I'm available on Mondays." _____

D Unscramble the words to form questions.

1. school / your child / like / does

_____?

2. what / does / your child / well / do

_____?

3. your child's / what / goals / is / one of

_____?

....

TAKE IT OUTSIDE: ASK A FAMILY MEMBER, FRIEND, OR COWORKER THE QUESTIONS IN ACTIVITY D. WRITE THEIR ANSWERS.

1. _____

_____

2. _____

_____

3. _____

_____

Unit 1: Setting Goals

Work: Reaching Your Goals

A Answer the questions. Use complete sentences.

1. What is your dream job?

_____

2. Do you think this is a dream that could come true? Why or why not?

_____

B Read the article. Then answer the questions.

Don't just dream—plan!

It is probably easy to imagine your dream job, but can you describe your plan for how to reach that job? Without a realistic plan, a dream job will never come true. Most people spend more time planning their next vacation than planning their career. It doesn't matter if you are still in school, or if you have been working for 15 years, now is the right time to set career goals and make plans.

1. Start by asking yourself questions. What kind of work do I want to do? What do I like about my current job? Who do I want to work with? What kind of place would I like to work in? How much do I want to earn? What job do I want to have in two years? What do I want to learn?

2. Think of some goals that you can accomplish in the next year. These should be goals that you can reach if you work hard.

3. Plan the steps needed to reach your goals. For each goal, write down three or four steps that you will need to take to reach the goal.

4. Look at your goals and the steps. Choose the ones that are the most important to work on in the next several months.

5. Make a timeline of your steps and goals. Plan steps for the next weeks and the next months. Every six months, evaluate your progress and revise your goals.

1. Why is it important to make career plans if you are still in school?

_____

2. Why should you make career plans if you are happy with your job?

_____

3. What new skill can you learn that can help you reach a career goal?

_____

4. Who do you know that can help you think about career goals?

_____

C Answer the five key questions from the reading. Give information about yourself. Then write possible ways you can accomplish your goals.

Key Questions from Reading	Your Goals	Steps for Reaching Your Goals
1. What kind of work do I want to do?		
2. How much do I want to earn?		
3. Who do I want to work with?		
4. What job do I want to have five years from now?		
5. What do I want to learn?		

D Choose one goal from Activity C. Make a timeline of steps that you can take over the next year to achieve that goal.

My goal: _____

Timeline for reaching my goal:

This week	In one month	In three months	In six months	In one year

Unit 1: Setting Goals

Practice Test

DIRECTIONS: Look at the pie chart below to answer the next five questions. Use the Answer Sheet.

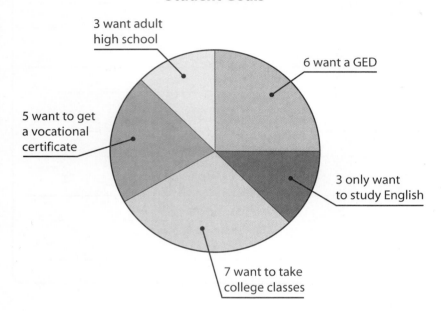

Student Goals

3 want adult high school

6 want a GED

5 want to get a vocational certificate

3 only want to study English

7 want to take college classes

ANSWER SHEET

1 Ⓐ Ⓑ Ⓒ Ⓓ
2 Ⓐ Ⓑ Ⓒ Ⓓ
3 Ⓐ Ⓑ Ⓒ Ⓓ
4 Ⓐ Ⓑ Ⓒ Ⓓ
5 Ⓐ Ⓑ Ⓒ Ⓓ
6 Ⓐ Ⓑ Ⓒ Ⓓ
7 Ⓐ Ⓑ Ⓒ Ⓓ
8 Ⓐ Ⓑ Ⓒ Ⓓ
9 Ⓐ Ⓑ Ⓒ Ⓓ
10 Ⓐ Ⓑ Ⓒ Ⓓ

1. What does the pie chart show?
   A. how much time students spend on their goals
   B. students' educational goals
   C. students' occupations
   D. students' ages

2. How many students want to get a vocational certificate?
   A. 3   C. 6
   B. 5   D. 7

3. How many students want to get a GED?
   A. 3   C. 6
   B. 5   D. 7

4. Which is the goal of the most students?
   A. to get a GED
   B. to take adult high school classes
   C. to take college classes
   D. to get a vocational certificate

5. Which goal do the smallest number of students want to achieve?
   A. get a GED
   B. study English
   C. take college classes
   D. get a vocational certificate

DIRECTIONS: Read the article to answer the next five questions. Use the Answer Sheet on page 18.

How to Succeed in School

You can do well in school if you follow certain steps. First, you should think about how you learn best. Do you like to see and read information? Then you may be a visual learner. Do you like to hear people tell you information? You may be an auditory learner. Do you learn best if you actually do something? Then you might be a hands-on learner. The following ideas can help different learners do well.

1. Take good notes to read later.
2. Ask questions.
3. Make a model.
4. Review information within 24 hours to remember it.
5. Don't give up.

---

6. Which strategy will help students who like to read information?
   A. 1
   B. 2
   C. 3
   D. 4

7. Which strategy will help students remember new vocabulary words?
   A. 1
   B. 4
   C. 5
   D. All the above

8. What should students do if they don't understand what the teacher says?
   A. take good notes
   B. ask questions
   C. practice
   D. review information within 24 hours

9. If students want to succeed, what should they do first?
   A. figure out how they learn best
   B. give up
   C. study every 24 hours
   D. follow the teacher

10. If you like to learn by doing, what advice is best?
    A. talk to the teacher
    B. make a model
    C. listen to tapes
    D. watch a video

HOW DID YOU DO? Count the number of correct answers on your answer sheet. Record this number in the bar graph on the inside back cover.

Describing a House

A Look at the photos. Complete the sentences about the houses with words from the box.

Jill's house

Rob's house

~~chimney~~	windows
front yard	trees
garage	porch
driveway	deck

1. Rob's house has a _____ *chimney* _____ but Jill's house doesn't.

2. Rob's house has a _____ and a _____ for his car, but Jill's doesn't.

3. Neither Rob's house nor Jill's house has a _____ in the front.

4. Both houses have some small _____ in the front.

5. Both houses have a lot of _____, so they are bright.

6. Jill's house a small _____ in front, but Rob's doesn't.

7. Jill's _____ is very large, but Rob's is not.

B Complete the sentences with words from Activity A.

1. I would like to keep my car inside, so a _____ is important to me.

2. Our letter carrier leaves packages on the front _____.

3. If the house has a fireplace, it must have a _____.

4. It's hot here in the summer. I'd like a house with _____ for shade.

5. My parents like to be outside, but they want to sit at a table. They would like a house with a _____.

6. When it snows we have to shovel the _____ before we can take the car out.

7. Right now our apartment is very dark. When we move, we want a house with a lot of _____.

C Look at the photo of Jill's house on page 20. Complete the paragraph with *a lot of, a few, many,* or *any*.

Jill likes her house because it is big. It has _____ room for her family, with _____ places for her children to play. They have their own bedrooms, and there is a room for Jill's mother-in-law. The house has windows on all sides, so it is warm and bright. There is a big back porch. Jill's family spends _____ time there. The backyard has a lovely fence, so the family dog can run free in the yard. There are _____ small trees in the backyard. But Jill's yard doesn't have _____ big trees—just _____ small plants out front. Jill's house doesn't have a garage, and there is no driveway. There aren't _____ sidewalks in her neighborhood, either.

D Write a paragraph and describe Rob's house from Activity A.

_____

_____

_____

_____

_____

_____

_____

_____

_____

_____

E Combine two words below to form compound nouns. Refer to Activities A and C.

back ✓	case	side
bath	drive	stair
bed	fire	walk
book	place	way
	room	yard ✓

backyard _____   _____

_____   _____

_____   _____

_____   _____

21

Understanding Housing Ads

A Look at the ads. What do the abbreviations stand for? Write the word next to each abbreviation.

SALE
A Home in Westwood area! 3BR/2BA, 2-car gar., wash/dry, elec, AC, fncd yd., $279,000. 310-555-5612
D CONDO—2BR, 1.5 BA, garden unit, w/d, pool, prvt. patio, $69,000. Located in Montebello. Call 562-555-0998

RENT
B HOUSE – 4 BR/2.5 BA, 2-car gar., fp, fncd, WD hookups. Pets ok. $825/mo. Available immed. 818-555-7612
E TOWNHOME—2 BR, gar., bk yrd, deck, W/D hookup., appls. Avail. immed. Near Cal State, Northridge. 818-555-1333

RENT
C APT FURN – Nice 1BR, 1 person, all util., elevator off-street prkg., laundry rm. sec. dep., Ref. $125 week. No pets. 818-555-1630
F APARTMENT – Cascade Circle, 2BR big yard, quiet nghbrhd, pch, appls., pets ok. $600/mo. Heat included. 323-555-4962

BR _____   util. _____

BA _____   dep. _____

AC _____   avail. _____

elec. _____   prkg. _____

B Read the following situations. Write the letter of the ad from Activity A.

I just moved to town. I'm planning on renting a small apartment for a few weeks until I know what part of town I want to live in. I'm not interested in paying more than $550 a month.

Which ad do you think Tan would like? _____

My husband and I are thinking about buying a house. We have a wonderful daughter, and we're planning on having another child soon. We also have a dog that needs a yard!

Which ad would Linda be interested in? _____

My husband died last year, so Buster and I live alone now. I'm thinking about moving to a two-bedroom apartment, but I need to have a yard for Buster. He's a great companion.

We moved here two months ago and we're staying with my brother. My wife is dreaming of moving to a house, but we can't afford to buy one yet. We want at least three bedrooms.

Which ad would Doris be most interested in? _____ Which ad would Martin be most interested in? _____

C Look at the ads in Activity A. Answer the questions.

1. How much is the rent for the two-bedroom apartment? _____

2. Are utilities included in the rent for the one-bedroom apartment? _____

3. Does the condo have a pool? _____

4. How much is the three-bedroom house? _____

D Complete the sentences with the gerund form of the verb in parentheses.

1. Ron and Nadia are thinking about _____*moving*_____ (move) to a new apartment.

2. Tom is concerned about _____ (find) an apartment with 24-hour security for his mother.

3. Hugo is planning on _____ (rent) a very small apartment until he saves enough money to move to a place he really likes.

4. I found an apartment I like, but I'm worried about _____ (have) enough money to pay the security deposit, the first month's rent, and the utility hookups.

5. Carlos and his wife dream about _____ (live) in a place with a big yard.

6. My parents are talking about _____ (sell) their house after they retire and moving to a small apartment in Phoenix.

7. Our daughter is very excited about _____ (get) her own bedroom.

8. I'm interested in _____ (live) with a roommate, so I am going to check the ads in the student newspaper.

Reporting Housing Problems

A Put the statements in order to make a conversation. Number them 1 to 9.

_____ Okay. I'll check it out as soon as I can.

_____ I can come around 2:30.

_____1_____ Hello. This is Ed.

_____ You're welcome. Good-bye.

_____ Yes. What can I do for you?

_____ Well, my air conditioner isn't working.

_____ Can you give me a more exact time?

_____ Hi. This is Sandra Peterson in Apartment 103B.

_____ That's great. Thanks. I'll see you then.

B Answer the questions.

1. Who is the tenant? _____

2. Where does she live? _____

3. Who is the landlord? _____

4. What is the problem? _____

5. What time will Ed come? _____

C Complete the form for the problem in Activity A. Use today's date.

> **Southside Property Management**
>
> Maintenance Request Form
>
> Tenant's name: _____   Date: _____
>
> Apt. # _____
>
> Description of problem: _____
>
> _____
>
> Date and approximate time of maintenance visit: _____

D Look at the photos. Describe the problem to your landlord or building manager.

This is your tenant in Apartment 7G. I'm calling to report

a problem with _____

_____

_____

_____

_____

_____

_____

TAKE IT OUTSIDE: INTERVIEW A FAMILY MEMBER, FRIEND, OR CO-WORKER. ASK THE THREE QUESTIONS BELOW. THEN WRITE A PARAGRAPH ABOUT THE PROBLEM.

1. What is one problem you had with your house or apartment last year?

2. Did you get help with the problem?

3. How was the problem solved?

_____

_____

_____

_____

_____

_____

_____

_____

25

Filling Out a Rental Application

A Read the article from a website. Then choose the correct answer for the questions.

⊗ ⊟ ⊞   RENTER'S INSURANCE

DEPARTMENT OF INSURANCE

Consumer Advice

Publications

Services

Consumer Issues

Company Lists

Complaint Info

File a Complaint

Look Up Company

Site Map

Look Up Agent

FAQ Search

Renter's Insurance

News reports of apartment fires often include **tragic** stories of renters who've lost everything because they weren't insured. A landlord's insurance usually covers the building, but not the personal property of residents. If you rent an apartment, duplex, or house, you may need renter's insurance to protect your **belongings**.

How Renter's Insurance Works
Renter's insurance is a type of residential property coverage specifically designed for people who rent houses or apartments. These policies are often called "tenant policies."

Renter's insurance
- pays to repair or replace personal property that's damaged, destroyed, or stolen. Limits on this coverage vary by policy, but most provide at least $4,000 worth of protection. Policies may limit payments for certain kinds of property. Common **maximums** are $100 for lost cash; $2,500 for personal property used for business; $500 for valuable papers; and $500 for theft of jewelry, watches, and furs. Renter's insurance also covers your luggage and other personal items when you travel for up to 10 percent of the amount of your policy or $1,000, whichever is greater.
- pays living expenses, such as motel costs, if you're **displaced** from your home or apartment. This "loss of use" coverage is generally limited to 20 percent of a policy's personal property coverage. For example, if you have $25,000 in personal property coverage, your loss-of-use coverage would be $5,000. You would be paid up to this amount for the reasonable time required to repair or replace your rented property.
- provides **liability** coverage if you are legally responsible for another person's injury or property damage. If someone is injured in your home and **files a lawsuit**, a renter's policy automatically provides $25,000 in liability coverage and pays your legal costs. Extra liability coverage is available for an additional premium.

1. What does renter's insurance cover?

   A. the tenant's things   B. the apartment   C. a car   D. medical problems

2. What is a common maximum that renter's insurance would pay for property used for business?

   A. $100   B. $500   C. $2,500   D. $1,000

3. When will renter's insurance help pay for motel costs?

   A. if you are injured   B. if you get a lawyer   C. if you have to leave   D. if you paid
                                                              because of damage   the premium

4. What does liability coverage pay for?

   A. someone injured in   B. loss of use   C. jewelry and furs   D. luggage on a trip
       your home

5. According to the information on the website, which amount of coverage is the largest?

   A. luggage   B. personal property   C. loss of use   D. lost cash

B Match the words from Activity A with the correct definitions. Use the context to guess the meanings.

Word	Definition
1. _____ tragic	a. the largest possible amount
2. _____ belongings	b. to take someone to court
3. _____ maximum	c. legal responsibility to pay
4. _____ displaced	d. things that you own
5. _____ liability	e. very sad
6. _____ file a lawsuit	f. forced to leave

C List the approximate amount it would take to replace your property. Write NA (*not applicable*) next to items you don't own.

Property	Replacement value
Furniture	
TV, VCR, Stereo, CDs, DVDs	
Computer	
Microwave oven	
Clothing	
Kitchenware	
Sports equipment	
Jewelry	
All other property	
TOTAL PERSONAL PROPERTY	

D Complete the word forms chart below with words from the reading.

Noun	Verb	Adjective
replacement person	_____	replaceable
_____	personalize	_____
	XXXXXX	liable
resident	reside	_____
reason	reason	_____

27

Reading: Previewing

A Look at the title of the article on page 29. Write another question based on the title. Then predict answers to the question.

Questions	Possible answers
1. What is a consumer hero?	Maybe it's someone who's a very smart shopper. Maybe it's someone who saves other people's money.
2.	

B Read the first sentence in each paragraph of the article and check (✓) the predictions you agree with.

Predictions

I think this article is about
- ☐ an immigrant who had a problem.
- ☐ someone who didn't have any money.
- ☐ someone who had a housing problem.
- ☐ someone who was treated unfairly.
- ☐ a landlord who had a bad tenant.
- ☐ someone who couldn't get help.
- ☐ someone who reported unfair treatment.

C Read the article and answer the questions.

1. How much money did Aslam Ahmed and his wife have in savings?

2. What happened when Mr. Ahmed tried to rent an apartment?

3. Why didn't Mr. Ahmed have a credit rating?

4. What did Mr. Ahmed do to solve his problem?

5. Did anyone help Mr. Ahmed? If yes, who helped him?

D Read the article quickly and then evaluate the previewing strategies. Answer these questions.

1. Were you able to correctly predict the topic of the article?

2. Which previewing strategy was the most useful to you?

3. Why does it help to preview an article before reading it?

Consumer Hero:
Aslam Ahmed

1 Aslam Ahmed is a Certified General Accountant who now works for Canada Customs and Revenue Agency. His wife, Christina, has worked in the private school system. But none of that mattered 12 years ago when the Ahmeds came to Canada from Bangladesh and settled in Mississauga.

2 The Ahmeds had $25,000 in savings and Christina had a job. But a landlord refused to rent to them because Aslam didn't have a credit rating—he had no history of paying with credit. The **assumption** was that Ahmed was a bad credit risk.

3 "It was terrible. I would not wish it upon my enemy to have a situation like this," Ahmed said. He had no Canadian credit history, because he'd just moved there. And elsewhere, he usually paid cash. "I never **defaulted** on any payments in my life and I couldn't believe it. I mean, why

4 He was so insulted he contacted an immigrant housing authority. With their help he took a risk as a newcomer. Ahmed complained. He argued that no credit shouldn't mean bad credit and that such an assumption was discriminatory.

5 The Ontario Human Rights Commission agreed. Leiloni Farha was Ahmed's lawyer on the case. "What the judgment says is that a landlord cannot use a lack of information as bad information," said Farha. This means that even if you don't have any credit, it doesn't mean that you have bad credit.

29

Writing: Writing a Complaint Letter

A Read the letter and answer the questions.

> Pier Street Apartments
> 923 Jackson Street, Apt. 14
> San Diego, CA 92113
>
> March 1, 2012
>
> Greta Wolf
> Pier Street Apartments
> 923 Jackson Street, Apt. 1
> San Diego, CA 92113
>
> Dear Ms. Wolf:
>
> I am writing to inform you that the lock on my front door is broken. It broke three weeks ago. I've called you several times and left messages on your answering machine, but you haven't called me back. I would like to buy a new lock and fix it myself. I will deduct the cost of the lock from my next rent check. Please contact me as soon as possible if you have a problem with this solution.
>
> Sincerely,
>
> *Henry Lu*

1. Who wrote the letter?

   _____

2. When did he write the letter?

   _____

3. What is the relationship between the letter writer and the recipient of the letter?

   _____

4. What is the writer's purpose for writing this letter?

   _____

5. What is the writer planning to do to solve his problem?

   _____

6. Do you think this is an effective letter? Why or why not?

   _____

B Read the letter and answer the questions.

Pier Street Apartments
923 Jackson Street, Apt. 27
San Diego, CA 92113

May 7, 2012

Greta Wolf
Pier Street Apartments
923 Jackson Street, Apt. 1
San Diego, CA 92113

Dear Ms. Wolf:

I am writing to let you know that I have a problem in my apartment. I knocked on your apartment door a few times this week to talk to you, but you weren't home. I also called you four or five times and sent you an email. I'd really like to get this problem solved right away.

Please call me or email me as soon as possible so we can discuss ways to solve my problem. If I don't hear from you by May 15, I'll pay to have the problem fixed myself and I'll deduct the amount of the repair from my next rent check.

Yours truly,

Mitchell Long

1. Who wrote the letter?

_____

2. What is the writer's purpose for writing this letter?

_____

3. What is the writer planning to do to solve his problem?

_____

_____

4. Do you think this is an effective letter? Why or why not?

_____

_____

C Write a letter of complaint to Greta Wolf about a problem in your apartment. Include the problem, how long you have had the problem, whether or not you have tried to contact Ms. Wolf about the problem, and what you plan to do.

Family: Safety at Home

A Look at the title of the article and the photos in Activity B. What do you think the article is about? Check the main idea.

☐ Children's furniture   ☐ Keeping your children safe at home   ☐ How to play with your baby

B Read the article. Check the childproofing tips that you follow now.

CHILDPROOF YOUR HOME

If you are expecting a baby or have small children in your home, you should childproof your home immediately. Look at your house from a toddler's point of view. Get down on the floor and look for dangers: places where a child could get a shock, a burn, or a cut.

Safety in the bathroom:

☐ Keep medications and cleaners out of the reach of children.

☐ Put non-slip mats in the shower and tub.

☐ Check the water temperature before you put your child in it.

☐ Supervise children under six years of age when they are in the bathtub.

☐ Keep electrical appliances away from the water.

Safety in the kitchen:

☐ Put childproof latches on cabinets.

☐ Keep electrical appliances and cords out of the reach of children.

☐ Turn pot handles away.

☐ Cook on back burners.

☐ Keep sharp knives in a locked drawer or out of reach.

☐ Supervise young children using the microwave.

☐ Don't carry hot liquids and a child.

Safety in the bedroom and living room:

☐ Cover electrical outlets with plastic covers.

☐ Wrap cords for curtains and blinds up out of reach.

☐ Keep small items out of reach so children won't swallow them.

☐ Put locks on windows.

☐ Use a child safety gate at the top and bottom of the stairs.

☐ Keep plants out of reach. Some are poisonous.

☐ Put padding on sharp edges such as the fireplace.

C Check *True* or *False*.

	True	False
1. You can see all the dangers in your house if you walk around.	☐	☐
2. You should put latches on cabinets so children can't open them.	☐	☐
3. You shouldn't cook on the back burners.	☐	☐
4. It's okay to leave small objects around the house.	☐	☐
5. The cords for blinds and curtains can be dangerous.	☐	☐
6. Microwaves are safe for children to use.	☐	☐

D Answer the questions using information from Activity B.

1. What are three things you can do so children don't get burns?

_____

2. What are two ways to prevent falls?

_____

3. How can you make sure children don't get a shock?

_____

E List three things you think new parents should buy to make their homes safer.

1. _____
2. _____
3. _____

....

TAKE IT OUTSIDE: INTERVIEW A FRIEND, FAMILY MEMBER OR COWORKER. WRITE THEIR ANSWERS IN THE CHART.

Children's names and ages	Dangers in their home?	How their home is childproofed

33

Community: Reading Utility Bills

A Read the utility bills. Then match the information.

SOUTHERN CALIFORNIA NATURAL GAS COMPANY
P.O. BOX 2445
LOS ANGELES, CA 90078

Please make check payable to SCNGC.
Return this portion with your payment.

Account Number	Billing Date			Thank you.
xxx09772x321	04/13/2011			
FOR SERVICE AT: 9413 FLOWER ST.			LOS ANGELES	
CURRENT CHARGES PAST DUE AFTER:		05/08/2011	TOTAL AMOUNT DUE	$66.00

Cable Television Company P.O. Box 83069 Los Angeles, CA 90013		Previous balance $30.00	Current charges $99.00	Total amount due $129.00	Payment due 04/29/11
Account Name J. Ritter	**Billing Date** 04/10/2011	Thank you for prompt payment. **Payments and adjustments** Balance last statement $99.00 Payment $69.00			
Account Number 198399837958937934808		**Curent Charges** Cable and Internet $90.00 Taxes $ 9.00 Total amount due $129.00			
Service address: 9413 FLOWER ST.		LOS ANGELES			
CURRENT CHARGES PAST DUE AFTER: 04/29/2011		TOTAL AMOUNT DUE $129.00			

1. _____ amount due on gas bill   a. $30.00

2. _____ date gas bill is due   b. $129.00

3. _____ amount due on cable bill   c. May 8

4. _____ date cable bill is due   d. April 29

5. _____ billing date for gas bill   e. $66.00

6. _____ balance of cable bill from March   f. April 13

B Read the information about using the telephone. Then answer the questions.

> For credit card, calling card, and collect calls, press "0" and then the 10-digit telephone number of the person you are calling. At the tone, enter your calling card or credit card number, or stay on the line for an operator.
>
> For direct calls, press "1" and then the 10-digit telephone number.
>
> Press 911 for an emergency.
>
> Press 411 for directory assistance.

1. What should you press for emergencies?_____

2. What should you press for directory assistance? _____

3. You want to call telephone number 619-555-0428. You have a prepaid calling card. What number should you press?_____

4. What is the first digit you should enter if you are calling directly? _____

C Read the conversation. Write the information on the lines. Then practice with a partner.

A: What city?

B: Los Angeles.

A: What listing?

B: Richard Harper.

Harper, Olivia 20013 Orchard Dr.	....	908-555-8945
Harper, Richard A 1400 Alameda St.	....	908-555-0783
Harper, Richard G 1920 S. Flower St.	....	973-555-0012
Harper, Steven S 7720 N. Wilshire	....	908-555-8945

A: Is that Richard A. Harper on Alameda or Richard G. Harper on Flower?

B: Hmm. I'm not sure. Can you give me* both numbers?

A: Please hold.

B: Oh, and sorry to bother you, but could I have both addresses as well?

A: One moment. The number for Richard A. Harper on

_____ is _____.

The number for Richard G. Harper on _____

is _____.

A: Thank you very much.

*Useful Expressions
to ask for information
Can you give me . . . ?
Could I have . . . ?
Can I get . . . ?
Let me have . . . , please.

Practice Test

DIRECTIONS: Read the housing ads to answer the next five questions. Use the Answer Sheet.

For Rent	For Rent
Area 1	Area 2
APARTMENT. Lrg. 3 BR, nr trans., small pets OK. Utils. Incl. $900/month. Call 555-8990.	SOUTH BAY. 4 BR house. Lrg. fncd yd. Pets OK. Modern & bright. New kitchen. $1000 + util, sec. Dep. 555-2340.
CONDO. 2 BR, 1 BA near NoHo Arts District. Prkg, patio. Newly remod., new carpet. No pets, No smoke. $875. 555-6777.	HOUSE. 3 BR, 2.5 BA. Pool, nice yd., 2-car garage. Nr Valley College & shopping. $1100. 555-9042.

ANSWER SHEET

	A	B	C	D
1	A	B	C	D
2	A	B	C	D
3	A	B	C	D
4	A	B	C	D
5	A	B	C	D
6	A	B	C	D
7	A	B	C	D
8	A	B	C	D
9	A	B	C	D
10	A	B	C	D

1. You are looking for a house to rent. Which area should you look in?
   A. Area 1
   B. Area 2
   C. Area 3
   D. Area 4

2. You want an apartment near a bus line or subway stop. Which number should you call?
   A. 555-8990
   B. 555-6777
   C. 555-2340
   D. 555-9042

3. You only want two bedrooms. How much is the rent?
   A. $900
   B. $875
   C. $1000
   D. $1100

4. You want a garage. Which ad meets your needs?
   A. apartment
   B. condo
   C. 4-bedroom house
   D. 3-bedroom house

5. You have a cat. Which ad is not appropriate for you?
   A. apartment
   B. condo
   C. 4-bedroom house
   D. 3-bedroom house

DIRECTIONS: Read the information about tenant's rights to answer the next five questions. Use the Answer Sheet on page 36.

> Landlords should maintain the property in a clean and safe condition. Leases usually state that the tenant has a responsibility to notify the landlord of any repairs needed. Even if there is no lease, a tenant should give the landlord notice of a problem because some defects can cause serious damage. For example, a water leak may damage ceilings, floors, carpet, and appliances. When you tell the landlord right away, the landlord is less likely to charge you for the repairs or deduct money from your security deposit. If you, as the tenant, are responsible for the damage, either because you caused it or you failed to report a problem, you may have to pay for the repairs. If it's an emergency such as a broken pipe, you should tell or call your landlord immediately. When you notify the landlord of a problem in writing, keep a copy for your records.

6. Why should you report problems immediately?
   A. A small problem can cause a lot of damage.
   B. The landlord may get mad at you.
   C. The lease says you have to.
   D. You don't get a security deposit.

7. When might you have to pay for a repair?
   A. The landlord doesn't make a repair.
   B. You don't have a lease.
   C. You caused the problem.
   D. It's a water leak.

8. What is a benefit of reporting a problem right away?
   A. The landlord is less likely to charge you for it.
   B. You will get a new lease.
   C. You get a copy of the notice.
   D. You get a new apartment.

9. In which situation would the landlord probably pay for the repair?
   A. Someone spilled tomato sauce on the carpet.
   B. Your son broke a window.
   C. There is a leak in the roof that is 8 months old, but you didn't report it.
   D. A pipe broke in the bathroom.

10. What are ways to notify the landlord of a problem?
    A. by phone
    B. in person
    C. in writing
    D. all the above

HOW DID YOU DO? Count the number of correct answers on your answer sheet. Record this number in the bar graph on the inside back cover.

Healthy and Unhealthy Behavior

A Take the survey. Check the things you do now.

How Healthy Are You?

_____ drink 6–8 glasses of water every day

_____ exercise at least 20 minutes, 5 days a week

_____ eat 4–6 servings of vegetables a day

_____ eat red meat only once or twice a week

_____ don't smoke

_____ wear sunblock or stay out of the sun

_____ don't drink soda

_____ limit the salt and sugar I eat

_____ sleep at least 7 hours a night

_____ always wear a seatbelt in the car

_____ check my blood pressure regularly

B Look at the photos. Name the activity and say if it is healthy or unhealthy.

1.

2.

3.

1. _____

2. _____

3. _____

C Cross out the word or phrase that has a different meaning.

1. ~~healthy~~   unhealthy   bad for your health
2. unhealthy food   healthy food   junk food
3. well-protected   safe   unprotected
4. sunbathing   relaxing   working
5. shade   sun   sunblock
6. exercising   wearing sunblock   drinking soda
7. helmet   life vest   glasses

D Complete the conversations with the words in parentheses. Use the present perfect of the verb.

1. A: My husband just called. He's sick. This is the first time he _____ (be / ever) sick, so I'm going home to see how he is.

   B: You're kidding, right? Everyone _____ (have) the flu or _____ (get) a stomach ache at some time in their life.

   A: Not my husband. He _____ (take / never) a day off from school or work before this week.

   B: Wow, he sure is lucky.

2. A: Hello Jack. What brings you in today?

   B: Hello Doctor Patel. I _____ (be) sick for the last few days.

   A: Hmmm. You have a fever and you have spots on your face. _____ you _____ (have / ever) the measles?

   B: No, I _____ (get / never) the measles or the mumps.

   A: Well, I think you have the measles now. _____ your children _____ (have) the measles yet?

   B: Yes, the younger one _____ (have) them all week.

   A: Well, that's probably why you have them now.

Understanding Medical Terms

A Read the article. Then, answer the questions with complete sentences.

Your Personal Medical History

You will probably have to fill out a medical history form every time you go to a new doctor. It's a good idea to have this information on hand. You should start now to gather the information before you will need it.

What to do: First, you should write down all your personal information, such as your name, date of birth, and insurance policy number. Then you should list any major health-related events (immunizations, surgeries, special procedures) and the dates they occurred, and your healthcare providers over time. You should gather any paperwork related to these health events, and collect contact information for the doctors.

What to include: In addition to your personal information and description of specific medical events, you will usually have to list any symptoms you have now, allergies, medications you are taking, your social or lifestyle habits, and some important information about family members (siblings, parents, grandparents, and children).

1. Why should you write up your personal medical history? _____

_____

2. What are some examples of significant medical events? _____

_____

3. For which family members should you have medical information? _____

_____

4. Why do you think you need to include information on medications you take? _____

_____

B Look at the form. Then, answer the questions below.

ADULT MEDICAL HISTORY FORM

(1) Name: _____ Age: _____

Insurance #: _____ Date of birth: _____

CURRENT MEDICATIONS

(2) Medication   Dose   How many times/day

_____

_____

(3) **ALLERGIES:**

_____

(4) **IMMUNIZATIONS:**

Hepatitis A _____ Hepatitis B _____ Measles _____

Rubella _____ Tetanus _____ Influenza _____

(5) **MEDICAL PROBLEMS:**

Please indicate if you have had any of the following (with dates):

☐ heart disease _____ ☐ high blood pressure _____

☐ diabetes _____ ☐ cancer _____

☐ stroke _____ ☐ high cholesterol _____

☐ depression _____ ☐ alcoholism _____

FAMILY HISTORY (check family members who have had the following):

Medical Condition	Mother	Father	Sister	Brother	Daughter	Son	Grand-father	Grand-mother
Asthma								
Cancer								
Heart Attack								
Diabetes								
Stroke								

(7) **SOCIAL HISTORY**

Do you wear a bike helmet?   ☐ Yes   ☐ No

Do you use seatbelts?   ☐ Yes   ☐ No

How do you rate your diet?   ☐ Good   ☐ Fair   ☐ Poor

Do you drink alcohol?   ☐ Yes   ☐ No   # drinks/week _____

1. In which section of the form would you write that you have diabetes? _____

2. In which section would you note that you have had a tetanus shot? _____

3. In which section would you indicate you are taking medication for high blood pressure? _____

4. In which section would you check that your mother had asthma? _____

C Complete the form with information about yourself.

Interpreting Medical Advice

A Read the conversation. Write the missing words.

> caffeine   complaint   don't   exercise   should   you

Physician: Hello, Mr. Waters. How are _____ feeling today?

Patient: Pretty good. My only _____ is that I can't sleep very well at night.

Physician: How much _____ do you drink each day?

Patient: Well, I have a couple cups of coffee in the morning and tea in the evening.

Physician: You _____ cut down on the amount of caffeine you drink. Also, what do you do just before bedtime?

Patient: That's usually when I go to the gym. I _____ for about an hour and a half. I thought that would make me tired.

Physician: Actually, exercise can wake you up. Why _____ you try exercising earlier in the day?

Patient: Okay, I'll give it a try.

B Answer the questions.

1. What's the patient's name? _____
2. What is his problem? _____
3. What two things might be causing the problem? _____
4. What is the doctor's advice? _____

C Match the problem and advice.

Problem

1. ____ "I feel nervous a lot."
2. ____ "I get really out of breath when I walk up stairs."
3. ____ "I'd really like to lose some weight."
4. ____ "I'm going to the beach tomorrow."
5. ____ "Around this time every year, I get a stuffy nose and itchy eyes."

Advice

a. "I suggest that you eat less junk food."
b. "I think you should reduce the amount of caffeine you drink."
c. "Why don't you ask the doctor about allergies?"
d. "I recommend that you get more exercise."
e. "You should wear sunblock."

D Complete the paragraph with the words in parentheses. Use the simple past or the present perfect.

I _____ (travel) all over the world and I _____ (see) many different
 ① ②

cultures and customs. Over the years, I _____ (be) very lucky, and I _____
 ③ ④

(get / never) sick on any trip. But last month, my luck _____ (change). I _____ (go)
 ⑤ ⑥

to Portugal for a two-week holiday. My first few days _____ (be) exciting.
 ⑦

I _____ (see) all the sights in Lisbon, and I _____ (eat) a lot of delicious Portuguese
 ⑧ ⑨

food. Then on my fourth day there, I _____ (wake) up with a high fever and a terrible
 ⑩

headache. I _____ (be / not) able to get out of bed. Luckily, I _____ (find) a
 ⑪ ⑫

doctor who _____ (speak) English and who _____ (come) to my hotel.
 ⑬ ⑭

He _____ (tell) me I _____ (have) a virus and that I _____ (need)
 ⑮ ⑯ ⑰

to stay in bed for a week.

....

TAKE IT OUTSIDE: INTERVIEW TWO FAMILY MEMBERS, FRIENDS, OR COWORKERS. ASK ABOUT A HEALTH CONCERN.
WRITE ONE SUGGESTION.

Name	One concern the person has about his/her health	Your advice
Toby	Wants to quit smoking	He should ask his doctor for help.

43

Finding Help

A Scan the information below. Find and underline the courses for the following topics.

1   domestic violence

2. communicating with teens

3. alcoholism

4. weight loss

5. drug abuse

Community Hospital Educational Services

The hospital has a wide variety of free courses about important health issues. For more information or to sign up for a class, call the Educational Services Offices at 555-1234.

Parenting Skills

Join us to improve your parenting skills. If your children are ages 4 to 12, this class will help you deal with conflict and improve your communication. Learn the best ways to discipline your children and how to build a stronger family. 6 sessions.

Weight Management Program

This program will help you develop a healthier lifestyle. Make changes that will lead to weight loss and improved self-image. You will learn about exercise, healthy eating, stress management, and strategies for maintaining a healthy lifestyle. 12 sessions

Nutrition for Health

Learn how a healthy, well-balanced diet can improve your physical and emotional health. We will discuss healthy eating habits, how to make better food choices, how to develop a healthy grocery list, healthy cooking, and lifestyle changes for better nutrition. 1 session

Teen and Parent Anger Management

Teens and parents can learn skills to manage angry feelings and behavior, and improve communication in the family. 5 sessions

Adult and Adolescent Drug Dependency Programs

Find the strength to help yourself or someone you love. Our outpatient drug abuse services are designed for adults, adolescents, and their families. During a 2-hour session, you will learn what resources are available and what classes are right for you. 1 session

Alcoholics Anonymous (AA)

If your relationship with alcohol has caused difficulties in your life, AA offers hope and opportunities for change. AA is a support group that has helped people quit drinking and start a new life. Ongoing.

Domestic Violence Support Group

This is an ongoing group for women who have experienced domestic violence. Learn how to increase your physical safety, recognize your strengths, and improve self-care. Members must be referred by a physician or social worker.

Smoking Cessation—Quit Now

In this six-session program, you will learn about addiction and how to design your own plan for stopping. Class members will receive free smoking cessation medications. 6 sessions

B Answer the questions with the names of the courses.

1. Which course meets for 5 sessions? _____

2. Which course meets for 12 sessions? _____

3. Which courses are ongoing? _____

4. Which course requires a referral from a physician or social worker? _____

5. Which courses help parents improve communication skills? _____

6. Which course includes free medication? _____

C Answer the questions with the information in Activity A.

1. Where are the courses offered?

_____

2. How do you sign up for a course?

_____

3. In which courses do you learn about a healthy diet?

_____

4. If someone is addicted to pain medication, which course would be best?

_____

5. Name two courses that are appropriate for a teenager.

_____

6. Is the Domestic Violence Support Group open to anyone?

_____

7. Can a family member attend the Adult and Adolescent Drug Dependency Programs?

_____

8. What three kinds of addiction are covered in the courses?

_____

Reading: Skimming and Scanning

A Skim the article and identify the topic. Then read the article.

The article is about _____.

The New (Thinner) Me
By Nancy Park

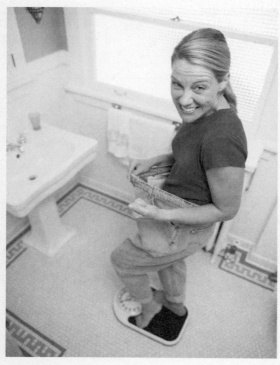

When I was a little girl, I was very thin. Then I went away to college and gained 20 pounds. I didn't exercise very much, and I ate a lot of junk food. Before that, I used to play basketball and run a lot, but in college I was too busy. After I graduated, I got a job in an office. I worked at a computer all day. At that time, my only excitement was going out to lunch. I gained ten more pounds.

Later, I met my future husband. One thing we really liked to do together was—you guessed it—go out to eat. We enjoyed all kinds of food, and soon, every one could tell.

Then I had a baby. I couldn't lose the extra 15 pounds I put on.

Last year, I noticed I was tired all the time, and I couldn't breathe very easily. I decided to get in shape. First, I talked to my doctor. She helped me work out a plan. Next, I joined a gym. I started an exercise program. I worked out three times a week. Then I changed my eating habits. I cut down on sweets and fatty foods and ate more fruits and vegetables. Because of these steps, I started to lose weight. It has taken me a year, but I'm 50 pounds lighter.

B Scan the article in Activity A to find the specific information below.

1. In college, Nancy ate a lot of _____.

2. After college, she worked in _____.

3. In her first job, she gained _____ pounds.

4. Nancy and her husband liked to _____.

5. Nancy worked out _____ times a week.

C Answer the questions about the article in Activity A.

1. What are three reasons why Nancy gained weight?

_____

_____

_____

2. What are three steps Nancy followed to lose weight?

_____

_____

_____

D Put the following events from Activity A in order from 1–7.

_____ Nancy got married.

_____ Nancy talked to her doctor.

_____ Nancy had a baby.

_____ Nancy played a lot of basketball.

_____ Nancy ate a lot of junk food.

_____ Nancy worked at a computer.

_____ Nancy exercised three times a week.

Writing: Compound Sentences

A Combine the sentences with *and* or *but* to make compound sentences.

1. I used to smoke. I don't anymore.

   _____

2. I don't drink. I watch what I eat.

   _____

3. I eat junk food sometimes. I don't drink soda.

   _____

4. I feel fine. I haven't had a check-up this year.

   _____

5. My family hasn't had any heart problems. My family hasn't had any cancer.

   _____

6. My brother had an operation. He is feeling much better now.

   _____

7. I used to have bad asthma. It has been better recently.

   _____

8. Megan's doctor gave her a prescription. She doesn't feel better.

   _____

B Complete the compound sentences with *and* or *but*.

Mario lives in Florida now, _____ he was born in Cuba. He lived there for 16 years before coming to the United States. After he came to the United States, he was stressed a lot, _____ he started smoking. He smoked all through college. Then Mario graduated, _____ he met a woman named Doris. Doris liked Mario, _____ she did not like his smoking. Mario decided to quit, _____ Doris married him. Mario used to like desserts, _____ he gave them up after he got married. He was surprised when he got diabetes. He started running, _____ that helped him control the disease. Mario has to continue exercising, _____ he has to continue to be careful of what he eats. He wants to be around for Doris for a long time.

C Read the pairs of sentences. Combine them to make compound sentences.

1. I decided to go on a diet.

   I look and feel better now.

   _____

   _____

2. He has started an exercise program.

   He is still eating a lot of junk food.

   _____

   _____

3. She fell off her bike.

   She hurt her arm.

   _____

   _____

4. I have never had a surgery.

   I have been in the hospital three times.

   _____

   _____

5. The company started a wellness program.

   Employees have been absent less.

   _____

   _____

E Write a paragraph about how you would like to change your habits to be healthier. Use at least one compound sentence.

_____

_____

_____

_____

_____

_____

Family: Children's Back-to-School Health

A Check the factors that you think may influence children's health and performance in school.

☐ height   ☐ weight

☐ how well they see   ☐ how well they hear

☐ allergies   ☐ how much they eat for breakfast

☐ what kind of backpack they carry

☐ what notebooks they have

☐ up-to-date immunizations

B Preview the article on back-to-school health issues. Were your answers in Activity A correct? Read the article.

Health Checklist for Back-to-School

The start of school is just around the corner, so now is the time to make sure your children are ready.

Can your child see and hear well? Many children don't succeed in school because they have vision or hearing problems that haven't been treated. Make an appointment to have your child's vision and hearing tested before the start of school.

Has your child had all the required immunizations? Children are not allowed to enter school without the necessary immunizations. Make sure their immunizations are up-to-date and that you have the record.

Have you updated your emergency information? Make sure your child and the school know how to reach you or another emergency contact at all times. List all necessary phone numbers.

Have you talked to your child about any other concerns? Is your child anxious or upset about anything related to school? Give children a little time to adjust at the beginning of the year, but if it continues to be a problem, have your child talk to a counselor at school.

Have you notified the school about other medical issues? Make sure the nurse knows what medications your child takes and about any allergies your child might have. Food allergies are especially important because of the food in the cafeteria and food brought by other children.

What are some other issues? Children who eat breakfast do better in school. Make sure that your child is not carrying a backpack that doesn't fit or is too heavy.

C Answer the questions using information from Activity B.

1. What must children have before they can enter school?

   _____

2. What problems might affect your child's performance in school?

   _____

3. What phone numbers should you give to the school?

   _____

4. When should your child talk to the counselor?

   _____

5. What information should you give to the school nurse?

   _____

6. What is one problem you see in the picture?

   _____

TAKE IT OUTSIDE: INTERVIEW A FAMILY MEMBER, FRIEND, OR COWORKER. ASK THE QUESTIONS BELOW. WRITE THEIR ANSWERS.

1. How many children do you have in school? _____

2. Have they all had vision and hearing tests? _____

3. Do any of your children have allergies? If so, what kind of allergies?

   _____

   _____

4. What concerns do you have about your children's health and school?

   _____

   _____

Work: Wellness Programs

A Answer the questions.

1. How can an employer help workers be healthier?

_____

2. Why should an employer be concerned about workers' health?

_____

B Read the website information. Check your answers for Activity A.

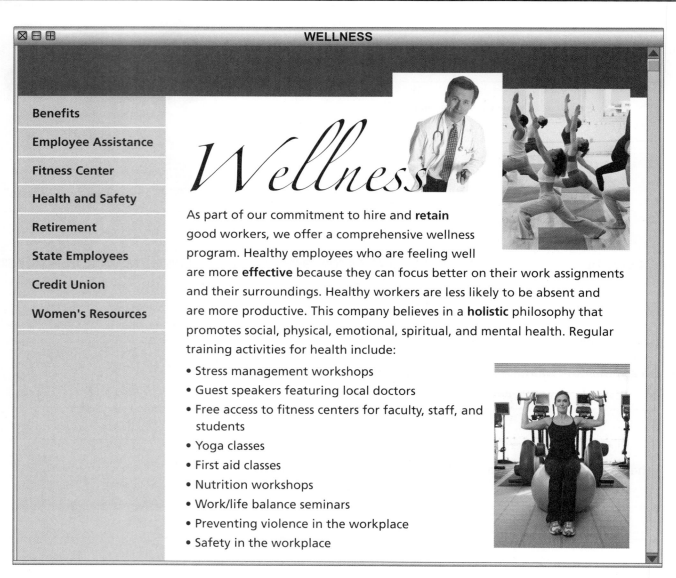

WELLNESS

Benefits

Employee Assistance

Fitness Center

Health and Safety

Retirement

State Employees

Credit Union

Women's Resources

Wellness

As part of our commitment to hire and **retain** good workers, we offer a comprehensive wellness program. Healthy employees who are feeling well are more **effective** because they can focus better on their work assignments and their surroundings. Healthy workers are less likely to be absent and are more productive. This company believes in a **holistic** philosophy that promotes social, physical, emotional, spiritual, and mental health. Regular training activities for health include:

- Stress management workshops
- Guest speakers featuring local doctors
- Free access to fitness centers for faculty, staff, and students
- Yoga classes
- First aid classes
- Nutrition workshops
- Work/life balance seminars
- Preventing violence in the workplace
- Safety in the workplace

C Circle the word or words with the closest meaning to the word in **bold**. Use the context.

1. As part of our commitment to hire and **retain** good workers, we offer a comprehensive wellness program.
   A. fire
   B. keep
   C. pay

2. Healthy employees who are feeling well are more **effective** because they can focus better on their work assignments and their surroundings.
   A. nervous
   B. tired
   C. able to complete work

3. This company believes in a **holistic** program that promotes social, physical, emotional, spiritual, and mental health.
   A. specific
   B. exercise
   C. whole

D Look at the different options in the wellness program on page 52. Rank the options from 1 (the most) to 9 (the least) in order of their interest to you.

_____ Stress management workshops

_____ Guest speakers featuring local doctors

_____ Free access to fitness centers for faculty, staff

_____ Yoga classes

_____ First aid classes

_____ Nutrition workshops

_____ Work/life balance seminars

_____ Preventing violence in the workplace

_____ Safety in the workplace

TAKE IT OUTSIDE: INTERVIEW A FAMILY MEMBER, FRIEND, OR COWORKER. WRITE THEIR ANSWERS.

1. What is the usual reason you miss work? _____

_____

2. What kind of health-related class would you be interested in? _____

_____

Practice Test

DIRECTIONS: Look at the nutrition label to answer the next five questions. Use the Answer Sheet.

Nutrition Facts

Serving Size: 9 cookies
Servings per container: about 5

Amount Per Serving

Calories	**140**
Calories from fat	50

	% daily
Total Fat 6 g	**9%**
Saturated fat 3.5g	18%
Polyunsaturated fat 1 g	
Monounsaturated fat 1 g	
Cholesterol 25mg	**8%**
Sodium 95 mg	**4%**
Total Carb 21 g	**7%**
Dietary fiber <1 g	3%
Sugars 6 g	
Protein 2 g	

Ingredients: Wheat flour, butter, sugar, whole eggs, baking soda, nonfat milk.

1. What are *ingredients*?
   A. the number of servings
   B. the different foods that are in the product
   C. how much the package weighs
   D. the name of the product

2. How many servings are there in the package?
   A. 9
   B. 50
   C. 5
   D. 140

3. How many calories are in one serving?
   A. 9
   B. 50
   C. 5
   D. 140

4. Which ingredient is in the smallest amount?
   A. wheat flour
   B. butter
   C. eggs
   D. nonfat milk

5. Which is the largest amount in grams?
   A. total fat
   B. total carbohydrates
   C. total protein
   D. sodium

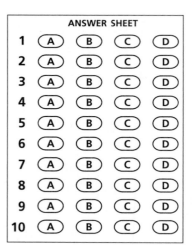

ANSWER SHEET

	A	B	C	D
1	Ⓐ	Ⓑ	Ⓒ	Ⓓ
2	Ⓐ	Ⓑ	Ⓒ	Ⓓ
3	Ⓐ	Ⓑ	Ⓒ	Ⓓ
4	Ⓐ	Ⓑ	Ⓒ	Ⓓ
5	Ⓐ	Ⓑ	Ⓒ	Ⓓ
6	Ⓐ	Ⓑ	Ⓒ	Ⓓ
7	Ⓐ	Ⓑ	Ⓒ	Ⓓ
8	Ⓐ	Ⓑ	Ⓒ	Ⓓ
9	Ⓐ	Ⓑ	Ⓒ	Ⓓ
10	Ⓐ	Ⓑ	Ⓒ	Ⓓ

DIRECTIONS: Look at the Health History Questionnaire and answer the questions. Use the Answer Sheet on page 54.

Health History Questionnaire

Date: 7 / 22 / 2013   Name: May Wong   DOB: 10 / 7 / 85

Medical Problems	Year Started	Surgeries	Date	Prescription Medications and Supplements / How Long Have You Taken Them?
asthma	1992	None		asthma medication /since 1992
nasal allergies	1993			allergy medication / since 1994
high cholesterol	2005			multi-vitamin /since 2000

Healthcare Providers: Dr. Ruiz, family doctor, & Dr. Lowe, dentist

Do you smoke? (X) Yes   ( ) No
How much alcohol do you drink each week? (X) None   ( ) 1 drink   ( ) 2 drinks   ( ) 3 or more drinks
Do you use illegal drugs?   ( ) Yes   (X) No

Please check the behaviors you follow:
(X) Wear a seatbelt   ( ) Smoke detector in house   ( ) Exercise more than 3 times a week
(X) Low-fat diet   ( ) Annual check-ups

Please check if you have a family history of any of the following:
(X) Heart disease   ( ) Skin cancer   (X) High cholesterol   (X) Asthma

6. Who is the patient's family doctor?
   A. Dr. Ruiz
   B. Dr. Lowe
   C. May Wong
   D. She doesn't have a family doctor.

7. Which of these does the patient *not* take?
   A. asthma medication
   B. high cholesterol medication
   C. allergy medication
   D. multi-vitamins

8. Which of these things does the patient *not* do?
   A. smoke
   B. wear a seatbelt
   C. eat a low-fat diet
   D. exercise more than three times a week

9. What disease is *not* in the patient's family?
   A. asthma
   B. high cholesterol
   C. heart disease
   D. skin cancer

10. When did the patient start taking allergy medication?
   A. 1992
   B. 1993
   C. 1994
   D. 2000

Making Purchasing Decisions

A Match the words or phrases to create collocations.

1. no money _____
2. certified _____
3. come with _____
4. lease _____

a. a warranty
b. pre-owned cars
c. down
d. or buy

B Complete the sentences with the gerund form of the verb in parentheses.

1. _____ (lease) a car can be a better idea than buying one.

2. _____ (pay) by credit can get people into financial trouble.

3. _____ (shop) online is very convenient.

4. _____ (pay) with cash is becoming old-fashioned.

5. _____ (own) a home is a big responsibility.

6. _____ (use) a debit card is the easiest way to pay for gas.

7. _____ (purchase) things when they are on sale saves money.

C Read the information about the televisions. Answer the questions.

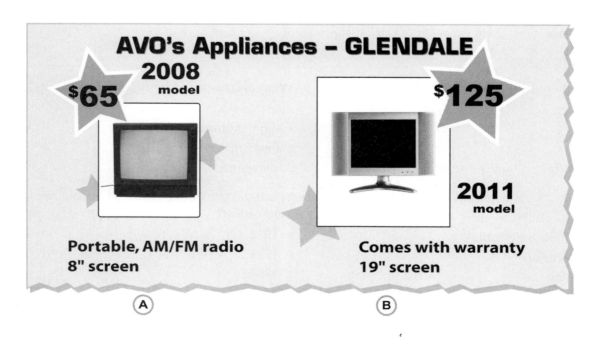

AVO's Appliances – GLENDALE

$65   2008 model

$125   2011 model

A Portable, AM/FM radio
8" screen

B Comes with warranty
19" screen

1. Which TV is newer? _____

2. Which TV is bigger? _____

3. Which is less expensive? _____

4. Which has a warranty? _____

5. Which one would you buy? Why? Give two reasons. _____

_____

D Look at the ads. Complete the Venn Diagram.

Whittier Lighting and Furniture

$23.99

Adjustable desk lamp
Comes with 1-year Warranty!
60 watt bulb

Ⓐ

$19.99

SALE

Reg. $25

Desk Lamp
Available in 5 colors
Uses a regular 60 watt bulb

Ⓑ

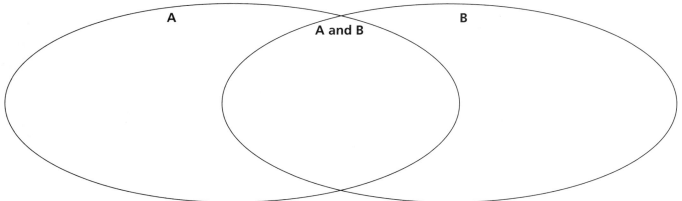

A

A and B

B

E Which lamp from Activity D would you buy and why? Give two reasons.

_____

_____

Warranties and Return Policies

A Scan the guarantee information to complete the sentences below.

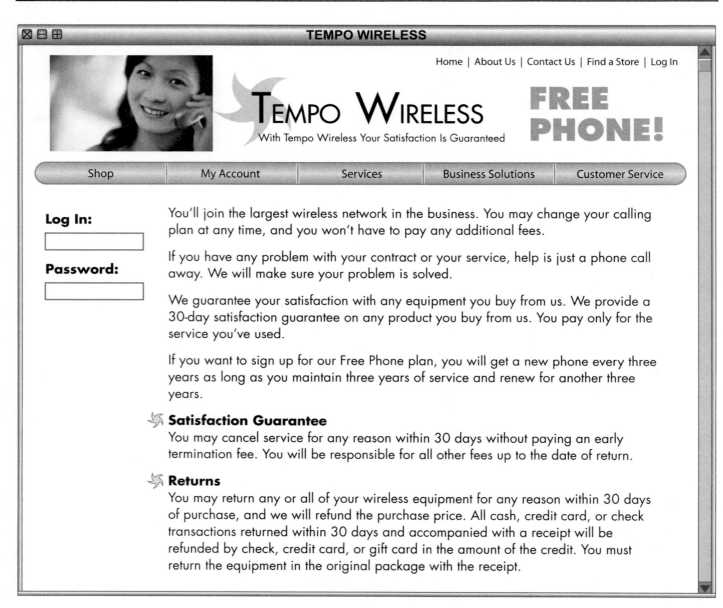

TEMPO WIRELESS

Home | About Us | Contact Us | Find a Store | Log In

TEMPO **W**IRELESS
With Tempo Wireless Your Satisfaction Is Guaranteed

FREE PHONE!

| Shop | My Account | Services | Business Solutions | Customer Service |

Log In:

Password:

You'll join the largest wireless network in the business. You may change your calling plan at any time, and you won't have to pay any additional fees.

If you have any problem with your contract or your service, help is just a phone call away. We will make sure your problem is solved.

We guarantee your satisfaction with any equipment you buy from us. We provide a 30-day satisfaction guarantee on any product you buy from us. You pay only for the service you've used.

If you want to sign up for our Free Phone plan, you will get a new phone every three years as long as you maintain three years of service and renew for another three years.

Satisfaction Guarantee
You may cancel service for any reason within 30 days without paying an early termination fee. You will be responsible for all other fees up to the date of return.

Returns
You may return any or all of your wireless equipment for any reason within 30 days of purchase, and we will refund the purchase price. All cash, credit card, or check transactions returned within 30 days and accompanied with a receipt will be refunded by check, credit card, or gift card in the amount of the credit. You must return the equipment in the original package with the receipt.

1. This company is the largest _____ network in the business.

2. Customers may change their _____ plan at any time.

3. The company provides a _____-day satisfaction guarantee.

4. With the Free Phone Plan, customers get a free phone every _____ years.

5. If you have a problem with your service, you should _____ the company or return the equipment to the store.

6. Customers need to return the equipment in the _____ and with the

   _____.

B Answer the questions using information from Activity A. Write complete sentences.

1. How long is the guarantee valid?

   _____

2. Does the guarantee cover defects in the equipment?

   _____

3. What two things do you need to do if you want a refund?

   _____

C Write affirmative or negative sentences that are true for you. Use the correct forms of the verbs in parentheses.

1. (enjoy / shop) I _____ during holiday sales.

2. (avoid / use) I _____ a credit card to pay for things.

3. (enjoy / make) I _____ big purchases.

4. (like / save) I _____ money with coupons.

5. (suggest / purchase) I _____ a pre-owned car rather than a new one.

6. (recommend / borrow) I _____ money from a friend rather than from the bank.

7. (recommend / open) I _____ a savings account for your children.

8. (suggest / read) I _____ the warranty carefully when you buy electronic equipment.

9. (avoid / give) I _____ my social security number over the phone.

10. (like / order) I _____ things online.

11. (enjoy / talk) I _____ about money.

Selecting a Car

A Put the statements in order to make a conversation. Number them 1 to 8.

_1_ Good afternoon. How can I help you today?

_____ That's good. What's the mileage on it?

_____ What kind of gas mileage does it get?

_____ How about this one? It's only a year old and it's a great price.

_____ I'd like to look at a small, pre-owned pickup truck.

_____ Just 40,000.

_____ It seems to me that that's a lot of miles on a truck that's only a year old.

_____ Almost 30 highway miles per gallon.

B Complete the questions with the comparative or superlative form of the adjective in parentheses. Then write an answer to the question.

1. Do you think a pre-owned car is a _____ (good) purchase than a new car?

_____

2. Do you think the mileage on the car is _____ (important) than the gas mileage?

_____

3. Would you prefer an SUV or a _____ (small) car?

_____

4. Do you think this year's cars are _____ (efficient) to drive than older models?

_____

C Read the warranty for the truck in Activity A. Remember the truck in Activity A is one year old and has 40,000 miles on it. Check *True* or *False*.

CERRITOS AUTO MALL
NEW VEHICLE WARRANTY

The chart summarizes coverage on your new car or truck.

Type of coverage	Years/miles
Car body parts	3/30,000
Rust	3/30,000
Engine	5/50,000
Seat belts	5/50,000

The coverage is for whatever happens first. For example, if you drive 30,000 miles before you reach three years, you are covered up to 30,000 miles.

Your dealer will repair or replace any defective parts during the period of coverage.

Certified Pre-owned Vehicle registered while under the New Vehicle Limited Warranty When the New Vehicle Warranty expires, the Certified Pre-Owned Vehicle Limited Warranty provides additional limited warranty for 12 months or 12,000 miles, whichever occurs first, from the date of purchase.

---

1. The truck is still covered by the New Vehicle Warranty if the engine fails.

   ☐ True   ☐ False

2. The truck is still covered by the New Vehicle Warranty if there are problems with the passenger side door.

   ☐ True   ☐ False

3. If the customer buys the truck, the Certified Pre-owned Vehicle Limited Warranty will cover any rust on the truck in the next three years.

   ☐ True   ☐ False

4. The Certified Pre-owned Vehicle Limited Warranty will provide up to one more year of coverage from the date of purchase for any problems with the seat belts.

   ☐ True   ☐ False

5. The Certified Pre-owned Vehicle Limited Warranty will provide up to one more year of coverage for any problems with the body parts.

   ☐ True   ☐ False

TAKE IT OUTSIDE: GO SHOPPING FOR AN EXPENSIVE ITEM SUCH AS A CAR, APPLIANCE, OR COMPUTER. ASK THE FOLLOWING QUESTIONS. HOW MUCH IS IT? DOES IT COME WITH A WARRANTY?

Unit 4: Money and Consumerism

Bank Services and Problems

A Check the services you personally need in a bank.

- ☐ Home loan or mortgage
- ☐ Savings account
- ☐ Checking account
- ☐ Check card

- ☐ Direct deposit
- ☐ Credit card
- ☐ Currency exchange
- ☐ Money orders

- ☐ Check cashing
- ☐ Overdraft protection
- ☐ Money transfers
- ☐ Car loan

B Complete the sentences with phrases from Activity A.

1. When you don't have enough money to buy a house, you can get a _____ from a bank.

2. It's useful to have _____ because then you are protected if you write a check for more money than you have.

3. Banks usually offer two types of accounts: _____ and _____.

4. Some people get a _____ from a bank when they purchase a vehicle.

5. Tourists often go to a _____ when they travel to another country.

6. If you have _____, you don't have to go to the bank every time you get paid.

C Read the information about banks and financial institutions on page 63. Then answer the questions.

1. Which type of financial institution is run by its members?

_____

2. Which financial institution specializes in mortgages?

_____

3. Which financial institution offers the most services?

_____

4. Which one offers the fewest services?

_____

5. Which one is probably the worst option for the consumer?

_____

⊠⊟⊞   **FINANCIAL INSTITUTIONS**

BANKS AND OTHER FINANCIAL INSTITUTIONS

| INSTITUTIONS | INVESTING | BUSINESS INFO | CUSTOMER SERVICE |

Commercial banks offer many services and products including savings and checking accounts, mortgages, and business and student loans. Commercial banks make a profit by providing loans and making investments.

Credit Unions are not-for-profit financial institutions. They are cooperatives run by the members. All "profits" are returned to the members in the form of lowered service fees and higher interest rates on savings accounts. Many people think they are as good as commercial banks (savings and checking accounts, loans). Some are specifically for immigrant populations, even those without documentation.

Savings and Loans started as a way to encourage saving and home ownership. They still specialize in mortgage or home loans, although they often offer savings and checking accounts too.

Currency exchanges do not accept deposits or make loans. They earn a profit by charging a fee for services such as cashing government checks or selling money orders. Their service fees are usually much higher than those of other financial institutions. Currency exchanges or check-cashing offices are often found in poorer neighborhoods.

D Answer the questions using complete sentences.

1. Why might some people not want to use a bank?

_____

_____

2. Why might some people not want to bank online?

_____

_____

Reading: Finding the Main Idea

A Write the main idea for each paragraph below.

1.   A new law means that your checks will be paid by your bank much faster than in the past. It used to take a couple of days for your check to clear. That meant that if you had insufficient funds, you could write a check today, deposit the money tomorrow, and the check would still be good. Now, however, because of the new law, banks don't have to send the original check to the customers' home banks. They now can send and accept digital, or computerized, versions of the check. This means that customers might bounce a check if they are counting on a two-day lag to get that check covered.

Main idea: _____

2.   The death of a spouse is perhaps the most upsetting time in anyone's life. The surviving husband or wife must make many changes in his or her life. There are many important financial decisions to make, and it can be a time of great financial stress. After the death of a spouse, survivors should put off making any major financial decisions, such as buying or selling a house. They should make sure they know of any benefits, such as life insurance. Also, survivors should make a monthly budget to account for sources of income and expenses.

Main idea: _____

3.   Fly Right Airlines has announced a new destination in the tropics. Starting October 18, the airline will fly to the Bahamas from Los Angeles twice a day. This will be a low-cost flight at only $175 one way. Fly Right is hoping that passengers will consider Fly Right when making vacation plans. This is the first time that Fly Right has offered a low-cost fare in a market where there is no competition.

Main idea: _____

B Look at the information below. Write a paragraph on how to manage student loans. Use the information below and your own ideas.

How to Manage Student Loans

- Keep a list of loans.
- Know how much you owe.
- Consolidate (combine) loans, so you only have to pay one.
- Shop around for low interest rates.
- Stick to a budget.
- Try to pay more each month.
- Repaying loans is hard, so you should not get angry if it takes a long time.

_____

_____

_____

_____

_____

_____

_____

_____

_____

C Write the main idea of the paragraph you wrote in Activity B.

Main idea: _____

_____

_____

Writing: Writing a Letter to Return Merchandise

A Match each problem with a reason for return.

a. It's defective.

b. It doesn't match the picture.

c. It's not as advertised.

d. It's the wrong color / size / type / model.

e. It's poor quality.

f. I don't like it. / I've changed my mind.

_____ 1. Lily bought an MP3 player online. She wanted the one with 30 gigabytes of memory and a large video screen, but the model that arrived in the mail had 20 gigabytes of memory and no video screen.

_____ 2. Luis ordered a chair from a catalog. In the catalog picture, the chair looked like it was made of wood. The chair that arrived was made of brown plastic.

_____ 3. Ming bought a jacket online. When she tried it on, she realized that it was very uncomfortable and didn't look good on her.

_____ 4. Carlos bought a television. The salesperson at the store helped him pick it out. When he got it home and turned it on, the picture wasn't clear.

_____ 5. Katy bought a jar of skin cream. The television commercial said that the cream would make her look five years younger in ten days, but after two weeks, her skin looks the same.

_____ 6. Peter bought a sofa. When it was delivered, he noticed that there was a large hole in the back.

B Number the sentences from a letter in the correct order. Write 1 to 6.

_____ In addition, your advertisement said the sweater was made of cotton, but this sweater is made of rayon.

_____ I would like to return the enclosed sweater for several reasons.

_____ Please refund my credit card for the full amount. Thank you.

_____ Secondly, there is a tear in one of the sleeves.

_____ First of all, the sweater looked heavy in the catalog picture, but it's very thin.

_____ Finally, it's not the color I ordered.

C Choose an item below. Then write four reasons why you might want to return it.

| a television | a pair of shoes | a sofa | a toy |
| a shirt | a computer | an MP3 player | a CD |

1. _____

2. _____

3. _____

4. _____

D Write a return letter. Use the information from Activity C and logical connectors.

_____ :

_____

_____

_____

_____

_____

_____

_____

_____

_____

_____

_____

_____

_____

_____

_____ ,

_____

Community: Car Maintenance and Repair

A Do you know these parts of a car? Check the ones that you know.

- ☐ battery
- ☐ brake lights
- ☐ brakes
- ☐ engine oil
- ☐ exhaust system
- ☐ headlights
- ☐ radiator
- ☐ tires
- ☐ turn indicator
- ☐ windshield wipers

B Complete the sentence. Use some of the words from Activity A.

1. When it is raining or dark outside, turn on your _____.

2. The _____ help to slow down or stop your car.

3. The _____ provides electricity to the engine.

4. Before a long road trip, check the air pressure in your _____.

5. To keep your car engine running well, you should put _____ in it every three to four months.

6. Use _____ when it is raining.

7. The _____ is inside the car, next to the steering wheel.

8. The _____ is filled with water and helps to cool the car engine.

C Match the problem to the solution.

____ 1. When I try to turn on the car, nothing happens. It doesn't start.

____ 2. One tire looks very low.

____ 3. I don't know how much air pressure my tires need.

____ 4. My brakes are very squeaky. They make a lot of noise.

____ 5. My "check engine" light is on.

a. You may have a slow leak. Check the air pressure, and then go to a gas station and add more air.

b. Have a mechanic check them.

c. Check your owner's manual. It has that information.

d. There may be a problem with your car computer. Drive your car to a mechanic.

e. The battery is probably dead.

D Read about car maintenance. Then answer the questions.

Car repairs can be very expensive and are often unexpected. If your car breaks down, you may have to spend hundreds of dollars to get it fixed. The best way to avoid expensive repairs is with regular maintenance. Good car maintenance will keep your engine in working condition and prevent problems. For example, if you check your oil regularly, you will know if the oil level is getting low. Car maintenance is also important for safety reasons. Good brakes, lights, and tires are important for safe driving. If you spend a little time and money to maintain your car, you can avoid some expensive repairs. When you plan your personal budget, be sure to include the cost of regular maintenance for your car.

Here are some basic maintenance tips.

- **Check your oil.** Add a quart of oil if the level is low. Change your oil and replace the oil filter every three months or every 3000 miles.
- **Check your tires.** Once a month, check the air pressure in your tires. Look at your tires to see if they are worn out. If they are, it is time for new tires. Most tires last for 40,000 to 60,000 miles.
- **Prepare for car trips.** Before a long trip, check your car fluids. For example, check the oil, windshield fluid, water, and air conditioning refrigerant.
- **Pay attention to any new or unusual sounds.** These can be a warning sign that something is wrong. You may need to take your car to a mechanic.
- **Get a tune-up once a year.** In a tune-up, the mechanic will check your car engine, replace fluids and parts, and make sure everything is in good condition.

For major car repairs, it is a good idea to get cost estimates from two different mechanics. Compare what each mechanic will do for the repair, and how much it will cost.

1. What are two reasons car maintenance is important?

_____

2. How often should you change the oil?

_____

3. How long do most tires last?

_____

4. What kinds of fluids are in a car?

_____

5. What is a tune-up?

_____

6. Why should you get estimates from two different mechanics for a repair?

_____

Family: Checking Accounts

A Read the information. Then complete the application for David Campos.

David Lorenzo Campos and his wife, Lori, want to open a checking account in their new town. They moved to Glendale only a month ago, but David has been working for Trillo's Toys at One Main Street in Burbank for six years now. They have saved $2,500 to open this account. Lori has trouble remembering some of David's personal information, so she writes down "000-40-1417" (his Social Security number) and "Matos" (his mother's maiden name). On the way to the bank, David reminds her to keep this and all of their other personal information in a safe place at home.

TRUE BANK

Checking Account Application

A True Bank Classic Checking account requires an initial deposit of at least $500. No minimum monthly balance is required. Checks are $15 a box. A Supreme Checking account requires an initial deposit of $5,000 and a minimum monthly balance of $2,500. Checks are free. Joint accounts are available for two people.

Account Ownership	Account Type	Opening Deposit
☐ single ☐ joint	☐ Classic ☐ Supreme	$ _____
_____ Last name	_____ First name	_____ Middle initial
_____ Mother's maiden name	_ _ _ – _ _ – _ _ _ _ Social Security number	06/25/1967 Date of birth
5094 Elm Street #8B Street address	91205 City, state, zip	Length of time at _____ current address
_____ Employer	_____ Employer's address	Length of time _____ employed

B After David opened an account at True Bank, he needed to pay his rent of $895.00 to his landlord, Hugo Loyola. Complete the check for David. Use today's date.

```
David L. Campos                                              072
  5094 Elm Street #8B
  Glendale, CA 91205              DATE_____

PAY TO THE
ORDER OF_____  $ [        ]

_____ DOLLARS

TRUE BANK
  CALIFORNIA
                              David L. Campos
MEMO_____
⑆012345678⑆   123⑈456 7⑈  0072
```

C Read the information about credit cards. Then complete the chart.

CREDIT CARDS: Are They a Good Idea?

Most adults in the U.S. have a credit card these days because it is very convenient. If you use a credit card, you don't have to carry around cash or a checkbook. You can shop online, avoiding the time and expense of going to the store. When you use a credit card and pay off your balance on time each month, you can avoid paying any fees and improve your credit score. However, the downside to using credit cards is real. Credit cards tempt consumers to spend much more money than they actually have, which leaves them with a lot of debt. The average American consumer owes about $8,000 in credit card debt! Most consumers end up paying a lot of money in interest because they do not pay off their balance every month.

balance: the total amount you owe for something (usually used when talking about one bill)

credit score: a number from 300 to 900 used by lenders to decide whether to loan you money; credit scores are based on your loan payment or credit card payment history.

debt: the total amount you owe (usually used when talking about all of the money you owe for several things you own)

downside: negative point, disadvantage

fee: extra money you have to pay based on a flat rate

interest: extra money you have to pay based on a percentage of the amount you owe

ADVANTAGES	DISADVANTAGES
don't have to carry cash	

Practice Test

DIRECTIONS: Read the ad to answer the next five questions. Use the Answer Sheet.

Tic Toc Time
North Hollyood
Watches
Reg. $24.99
Now $19.99
Save 20%

Shop online for selected items.

1. What items are on sale?
   A. selected items
   B. entire stock
   C. watches
   D. online

2. According to the ad, what is the original price of the watch?
   A. $20
   B. $24.99
   C. $19.99
   D. $200

3. What is the sale price?
   A. $20.00
   B. $19.99
   C. $24.99
   D. $22.99

4. How much will you save if you buy the watch on sale?
   A. $20.00
   B. $24.99
   C. $19.99
   D. $5.00

5. About how much would the watch cost at 40% off?
   A. $14.99
   B. $10.99
   C. $20.00
   D. $15.99

DIRECTIONS: Read the warranty below to answer the next five questions. Use the Answer Sheet on page 72.

Limited Warranty

Your coffeemaker is covered by the following warranty.

If your coffeemaker does not work because of defects in materials or workmanship, we will repair or replace the coffeemaker. This warranty will be void if the problem is due to accident or misuse.

The warranty is valid for one year from date of purchase.

Purchaser must supply a receipt to prove date of purchase.

---

6. What product is the warranty for?
   A. a vacuum
   B. a car
   C. a coffeemaker
   D. a camera

7. What is the period of coverage?
   A. a receipt
   B. a refund
   C. void
   D. one year

8. What is NOT covered?
   A. damage due to an accident
   B. defects in materials
   C. defects in workmanship
   D. the coffeemaker

9. What will the company do if the coffeemaker is under warranty?
   A. refund the money
   B. repair the coffeemaker
   C. replace the coffeemaker
   D. either B or C

10. What does the customer need to give the company?
   A. the receipt with date of purchase
   B. his telephone number
   C. the original package
   D. the receipt and original package

HOW DID YOU DO? Count the number of correct answers on your answer sheet. Record this number in the bar graph on the inside back cover.

Identifying Safety Hazards

A Look at the pictures. Identify the workplace safety equipment. Write the words from the box under the pictures.

> coveralls   gloves   safety vest   hard hat   safety goggles   face mask

1. _____

2. _____

3. _____

4. _____

5. _____

6. _____

B Complete the sentences with the past continuous form of the verb in parentheses.

1. Luckily, Sue _____ (wear) safety goggles when the chemicals exploded.

2. While we _____ (paint) the house, my friend fell off the ladder.

3. Sadly, the nurse _____ (pay attention / not) during the operation.

4. Jim _____ (wait) at the construction site when we arrived.

5. Some of the workers _____ (use / not) the proper safety equipment when the boss showed up.

C Read the memo.

> **Superior Auto Parts**
> **Van Nuys, CA 91406**
> # MEMO
>
> **To:** All Employees
> **From:** Lilia Banks, Vice President
> **Re:** Workplace Safety
>
> In an effort to improve safety in the workplace, we are asking employees on all shifts to observe the following rules.
>
> 1. Employees should wear safety goggles at all times when they are working in the production area. Sparks from the machines can injure eyes.
> 2. Employees must wear safety harnesses when working on scaffolding.
> 3. Employees in Shipping and Receiving must wear hard hats when working in the loading dock area.

D Write questions about the memo. Then answer the questions you wrote.

1. Who _____?

   Answer: _____

2. When _____?

   Answer: _____

3. Why _____?

   Answer: _____

4. Where _____?

   Answer: _____

E Match the appropriate preventive measure to each potential hazard below.

Preventive Measure	Hazard
1. _____ Wear safety goggles	a. so chemicals don't get in your food.
2. _____ Don't eat and drink in the work area	b. so chemicals don't get in your eyes.
3. _____ Wear protective clothing	c. to protect your clothing.
4. _____ Keep hands away from machinery	d. or you could cut your finger.
5. _____ Use earplugs	e. because spills can cause falls.
6. _____ Wear coveralls	f. so the loud machines don't hurt your hearing.

Identifying Accidents and Emergencies

A Check the situations below that you think are emergencies.

☐ You fractured a finger.

☐ There is a fire in a trash can.

☐ You have an intense pain in your chest.

☐ A thunderstorm is coming.

☐ You got a dent in your car door.

☐ You witnessed a bad car accident.

☐ Your child drank a toxic household cleaner.

☐ You are locked out of your house.

☐ Your child has an eye injury.

☐ Someone robbed you.

☐ Your spouse loses consciousness.

☐ You hear an explosion.

B Complete the sentence with your definition of *emergency.*

An emergency is _____

_____

C Look at the signs below. Write the letter of the sign next to the potential emergency.

a.

b.

c.

d.

e.

1. _____ Someone could get a bad shock.

2. _____ Materials could catch fire or explode.

3. _____ Someone could fall down.

4. _____ These materials are toxic.

5. _____ A train may cross the road and hit a car.

D Complete the sentences with the simple past or the past continuous form of the verb in parentheses.

1. Paul _____ (wear / not) safety a helmet when he _____ (fall) from the scaffolding.

2. While we _____ (go) through the intersection, a sports car _____ (run) the light and _____ (hit) our car from the side.

3. Jack _____ (inspect) the machine when it _____ (explode).

4. Barry _____ (drop) the beam while he and Nancy _____ (carry) it to the building.

5. Mack _____ (lose) consciousness when he _____ (fall) off the ladder.

6. Susan _____ (ski) when she _____ (fracture) her leg.

7. The painters _____ (paint) while the electricians _____ (install) new wiring.

8. A bee _____ (fly) into my eye while I _____ (eat) lunch.

E Circle the letter of the correct answer.

1. I have to buy a new computer. I was the victim of a _____.
   A. robbery   B. rob   C. robbed

2. There was a gas leak at the factory. They thought something might _____.
   A. explosion   B. explode   C. explosive

3. She has a terrible rash. She thinks she touched something _____.
   A. toxin   B. intoxicate   C. toxic

4. A hurricane is coming, so the governor ordered an _____.
   A. evacuation   B. evacuate   C. evacuated

5. It was so hot yesterday. Matt had heat _____.
   A. exhaustion   B. exhaust   C. exhaustive

6. I saw a car accident. Three people were _____.
   A. injury   B. injure   C. injured

Reporting Accidents

A Match the employee's responses to the supervisor's questions. Write the letter on the line.

Hector Lopez (supervisor):

1. _____ How's your eye?
2. _____ Can you tell me what you got in your eye?
3. _____ When did it happen?
4. _____ How did it happen?
5. _____ Were you wearing safety goggles?
6. _____ Why not? You know it's a rule.
7. _____ Did you fill out an accident report?

Tim Johnson (employee):

a. I was repairing some wires when they caught on fire.

b. It's better, thanks.

c. No, I wasn't.

d. I forgot to get them before I worked on the wires. Sorry. I'll be more careful in the future.

e. Not yet. I'll do that right away.

f. Smoke and dust particles.

g. Yesterday, around 3:00.

B Complete the accident report for the incident in Activity A. Use today's date on the form.

ACCIDENT REPORT

Name of employee injured: _____

Date of injury: _____   Time of injury: _____

Body part injured: _____

Type of injury: _____

How did the injury happen: _____

_____

_____

Name of supervisor: _____

Date of report: _____

C   Look at the picture below. Pretend you are the injured person. Answer the questions.

1. What happened?

   _____

2. What were you doing when it happened?

   _____

3. What did you injure?

   _____

4. What will you do next time to prevent an accident?

   _____

   _____

D   Complete the questions with the correct form of the verb. Then write answers.

1. Have you ever _____ (have) an accident at work?

   _____

2. What _____ (happen)?

   _____

   _____

3. Where _____ you _____ (work) when it happened?

   _____

4. What _____ you _____ (do) when it happened?

   _____

   _____

5. Who _____ you _____ (work) with when it happened?

   _____

TAKE IT OUTSIDE: INTERVIEW A FAMILY MEMBER, FRIEND, OR COWORKER. ASK THE QUESTIONS IN ACTIVITY D. WRITE A PARAGRAPH ABOUT THE ACCIDENT.

_____

_____

_____

_____

_____

First Aid

A Review your knowledge of first aid. Complete the chart.

Problem	You should	You shouldn't
1. Your son fell and broke his wrist. He also cut his leg, and it is bleeding.		
2. Your mother was working in the garden in the hot sun. Now she has heat exhaustion.		
3. Your friend spilled some hot water on her arm. Her arm is red and there are small blisters on it.		
4. Your daughter was washing the windows and she got some window cleaner in her eye.		

B Match the *if* clause with the result clause.

If clause

1. _____ If John has to work with toxic liquids,
2. _____ If you work around loud noises,
3. _____ If a worker gets burned,
4. _____ If someone is bleeding a lot,
5. _____ If they stand on their feet all day,
6. _____ If we don't clean up the spill on the floor,
7. _____ If you work on scaffolding,
8. _____ If your child swallows cleanser,

Result clause

a. he'll wear gloves.
b. someone might slip.
c. you must wear a safety harness.
d. you'll take her to the emergency room.
e. we will apply pressure on the wound
f. they should wear good boots.
g. we will put the injured area in cold water.
h. you should wear ear plugs.

C Read the instructions. Then, answer the questions in complete sentences.

FIRST AID

Sprains, strains and tears
- Apply cold packs or a small bag of ice wrapped in a cloth (30 minutes on, 30 minutes off) to reduce swelling.
- Wrap the joint with a supporting bandage.
- Keep the affected limb elevated.

Bruises
- Apply cold compresses or an ice pack.
- If bruise is on an arm or leg, elevate the limb.
- After 24 hours, apply a warm wet compress.

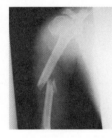

Fractures
- If the fracture is severe or open (broken bone coming through a cut in the skin), call 911.
- If it is not severe, take the victim to a hospital or doctor's office.
- Do not move the injured body part. Try to keep it immobile.

1. Which injuries will benefit if you put ice on them?

_____

2. What number should you call if a fracture is severe?

_____

3. Will swelling be increased if you put a cold pack on a sprain?

_____

4. When should you elevate an arm or leg?

_____

5. How long should you keep an ice pack on a strain?

_____

Reading: Using the SQ3R Strategy

A **Survey.** Survey the article on page 83. Answer the questions.

1. What job do you think this reading is about?

   _____

2. What are two adjectives that you think describe this job?

   _____

B **Question.** Write three questions that you think the article might answer.

1. _____?

   Answer: _____

2. _____?

   Answer: _____

3. _____?

   Answer: _____

C **Read.** Read the article and answer the questions in Activity B, if possible.

D **Recite.** Tell a partner about the article or repeat it to yourself. Write two sentences.

_____

_____

_____

_____

E **Review.** Reread the article. Write two things the writer likes and one thing he doesn't like about his job.

Likes: _____

Likes: _____

Dislikes: _____

The Life of a Paramedic

I have been a paramedic for several years, and I really like my job most of the time. To become a paramedic, you need two years of specialized training. I completed a certificate program at the local community college. I learned a lot, but school couldn't prepare me completely for the life of a paramedic which is exciting, rewarding, and stressful.

One thing I really like about my job is that it is not routine. We travel all over the city, and you never know what you will be doing from one hour to the next. We treat all kinds of medical emergencies. I learn something new every day.

Being a paramedic is very rewarding. I've always wanted a career in medicine because I like to help other people and I enjoy science. As a paramedic, I help people all the time: drivers in car accidents, elderly people who have heart attacks, and children who fall on the playground. My patients can't always thank me, but I'm happy when I can assist them.

The major disadvantage of the job is the stress. Paramedics deal with life and death situations all the time. Although it is rewarding to help someone, we aren't always successful. Sometimes a patient dies. We also have to work very quickly, and that can be stressful, too. We deal with people who are hurt and in trouble, and sometimes they are very stressed, too.

F Write a paragraph about a job that interests you. Use the article as a model.

_____

_____

_____

_____

_____

_____

_____

_____

_____

Writing: Making a Venn Diagram

A Read the paragraph and complete the Venn Diagram.

Hurricanes or blizzards? Take your pick. No matter where you live, you will probably have bad weather some time. In the northeastern United States, summers are often pleasant, but winters can be cold and snowy. Some winter storms, or blizzards, can dump up to several feet of snow. Temperatures can go below 0° Fahrenheit (–18° Celsius). In the southeastern United States, winters are nice and relatively warm, but summers bring their own danger. Hurricanes, with wind speeds over 100 miles (161 kilometers) an hour and a lot of rain, frequently hit Florida and nearby states. Both areas of the country experience weather emergencies and may lose power during a bad storm.

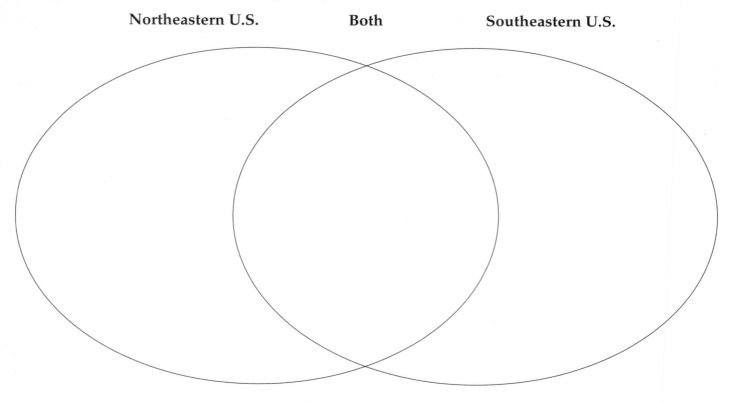

Northeastern U.S.   Both   Southeastern U.S.

B Think about home and workplace safety. Compare possible dangers at work and at home. Take notes in the Venn Diagram below.

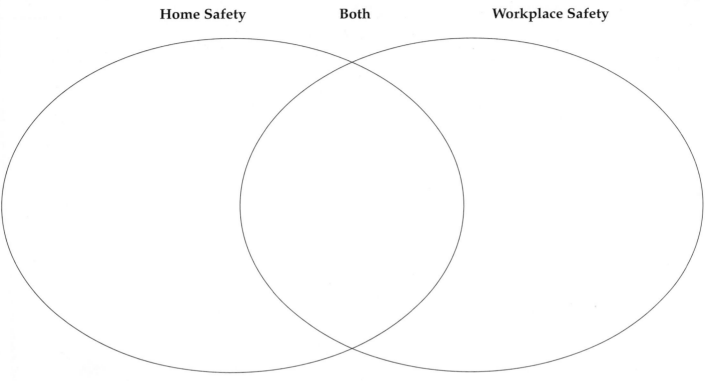

Home Safety   **Both**   **Workplace Safety**

C Write a paragraph comparing home and workplace dangers you chose for Activity B.

_____

_____

_____

_____

_____

_____

_____

_____

_____

_____

Family: Preparing for an Emergency

A Preview the website information in Activity B to find the main idea.

1. What is the main idea?

   A. You are ready for emergencies.

   B. You can get ready for emergencies by doing certain things.

   C. Emergencies are stressful.

   D. Change your batteries.

B Read the information from a government website (www.citizencorps.gov) about how you can be safer. Check the things you already do.

ARE YOU READY?

❑ 1. Check and change the batteries in your smoke alarms and replace all alarms that are more than 10 years old.

❑ 2. Make sure you know where your local fire department, police station, and hospital are and post a list of emergency phone numbers near all the telephones in your home.

❑ 3. Organize and practice a family fire drill—make sure your children know what your smoke detector sounds like, what to do if it goes off, and where to meet outside the house.

❑ 4. Locate the utility mains (gas, electricity, and water) for your home in case you have to leave, and be sure you know how to turn them off manually.

❑ 5. Create an emergency plan for your household, including your pets. Decide where your family will meet if a disaster does happen: (1) right outside your home in case of a sudden emergency like a fire, and (2) outside your neighborhood in case you can't return home—ask an out of town friend to be your "family contact" to relay messages.

❑ 6. Check expiration dates of all over-the-counter medications—discard all that are expired and replace any that are routinely needed.

❑ 7. Make sure all cleaning products and dangerous objects are out of children's reach.

C Write the number of the tasks from the reading under the appropriate headings in the chart. You may write a task in more than one place.

To be ready for a fire	To prevent medical emergencies	To be ready to evacuate

D Answer the questions about you.

1. Do you have smoke detectors in your home? Where are they? _____

_____

2. Where is the closest hospital to your home? _____

3. What medications do you and your family members use? _____

_____

4. Where will your family or friends meet outside the neighborhood if there is an emergency? _____

_____

TAKE IT OUTSIDE: INTERVIEW SOMEONE WHO IS NOT IN YOUR FAMILY. ASK THE QUESTIONS IN ACTIVITY D. WRITE A PARAGRAPH IN THE SPACE BELOW AND GIVE THAT PERSON SUGGESTIONS ABOUT HOW HE OR SHE CAN GET READY FOR AN EMERGENCY.

_____

_____

_____

_____

_____

Community: Getting Out of a Building

A Read the information from www.ready.gov.

1. Use available information to evaluate the situation. Note where the closest emergency exit is.

2. Be sure you know another way out of the building in case your first choice is blocked.

3. Take cover under a desk or table if things are falling.

4. Move away from file cabinets, bookshelves or other things that might fall.

5. Face away from windows and glass. Move away from exterior walls.

6. Determine if you should stay put, "shelter-in-place" or get away. Listen for and follow instructions from authorities.

7. Take your emergency supply kit, unless there is reason to believe it has been contaminated.

8. Do not use elevators.

9. Stay to the right while going down stairwells to allow emergency workers to come up the stairs into the building.

Source: www.ready.gov

B Match the sentence to the correct box from Activity A. Write the number on the line.

_____ When you go downstairs, walk on the right.

_____ Don't stand by objects that may fall.

_____ Listen for directions on what to do.

_____ Know where the closest emergency exit is.

_____ Use the stairs.

_____ Take all emergency supplies with you.

_____ Don't stand by windows.

_____ If things may fall on you, get under furniture.

_____ Know where all the exits are.

C Answer the questions in complete sentences.

1. How many times a week are you in a big building?

_____

_____

2. How often do you use an elevator?

_____

_____

3. Where are the closest emergency exits at your school or work?

_____

_____

TAKE IT OUTSIDE: INTERVIEW A FAMILY MEMBER, FRIEND, OR COWORKER. ASK THE QUESTIONS IN ACTIVITY C. THEN, ANSWER THE QUESTIONS BELOW.

1. Which of you is in a big building more often? _____

2. Who uses an elevator more often? _____

Practice Test

DIRECTIONS: Look at the accident report below to answer the next five questions. Use the Answer Sheet.

Quick Print   Wilmington, CA

ACCIDENT REPORT

(1) Name of employee injured: _Alina Mann_

(2) Date of injury: _12/02/12_   Time of injury: _12:30 p.m._   **(3)**

(4) Body part injured: _right hand_
Type of injury: _cut_

(5) How did the injury happen: _Alina Mann was operating the printing machine_
when the machine jammed. She tried to free the jam, but she forgot to
turn the machine off.

(6) Name of supervisor: _Terry Jones_
Date of report: _12/03/12_

---

1. Who got hurt?
   A. Alina Mann
   B. Terry Jones
   C. right hand
   D. cut

2. What was she doing at the time of the accident?
   A. She was printing.
   B. She was cutting.
   C. She was operating a machine.
   D. She was trying to free the jam in the machine.

3. Where on the form do you write the time of the accident?
   A. Part 1
   B. Part 2
   C. Part 3
   D. Part 4

4. Where do you write the date the form was completed?
   A. Part 2
   B. Part 3
   C. Part 5
   D. Part 6

5. What did she hurt?
   A. her right hand
   B. her left hand
   C. her cut
   D. a jam

	ANSWER SHEET			
1	A	B	C	D
2	A	B	C	D
3	A	B	C	D
4	A	B	C	D
5	A	B	C	D
6	A	B	C	D
7	A	B	C	D
8	A	B	C	D
9	A	B	C	D
10	A	B	C	D

DIRECTIONS: Read the article about first aid to answer the next five questions. Use the Answer Sheet on page 90.

Head Injuries

1. Check for bleeding. If there is severe bleeding, apply pressure with a sterile bandage to stop the bleeding.

2. If the person is conscious and alert, put an ice pack on the injury to reduce swelling. Make sure you wrap the ice or ice pack in a cloth before you put it on the skin.

3. Watch the person with the head injury for 24 hours. If there are any signs of concussion, call a doctor immediately. A concussion is a bruise to the brain. If breathing or skin color changes, or if the injured person appears confused and disoriented, call a doctor.

6. What should you do if there is bleeding?
   A. Call 911.
   B. Apply an ice pack.
   C. Apply pressure with a sterile bandage.
   D. Wrap ice in a cloth.

7. What should you do to the ice pack before you put it on the skin?
   A. Call 911.
   B. Call your doctor.
   C. Wrap the ice pack in a cloth.
   D. Apply pressure.

8. What is a concussion?
   A. a cut
   B. an injury to the brain
   C. a bruise on the head
   D. pressure

9. When should you call the doctor?
   A. if there is a cut
   B. if the injured person's breathing changes
   C. if you need ice
   D. if there is swelling

10. How long should you watch the injured person?
    A. for one day
    B. for 2 hours
    C. for 2 weeks
    D. until he or she falls asleep

HOW DID YOU DO? Count the number of correct answers on your answer sheet. Record this number in the bar graph on the inside back cover.

Unit 6: Community

Identifying Community Issues

A Look at the table below that compares the qualities of two cities in the United States. Answer the questions.

Feature		Louisville, CO	Keller, TX
Weather	High temperature Low temperature	86°F 17.5°F	95.6°F 32.4°F
Financial	Median income* Sales tax Auto insurance Home price	$102,600 3.00% $1,514 $310,000	$110,000 6.25% $1,514 $266,000
Culture (within 30 miles)	Libraries Museums Restaurants	37 7 2,104	59 8 3,144
Population	Median age	36.6	34.9
Crime	Personal crime risk† Property crime risk	1 15	0 14
Education	(within 30 miles) Colleges, universities Job Growth Average Commute	 20 −3.13% 19.5 min.	 19 58.76% 21.6 min.

*national average: $50,233   †based on 100 average, lower is better   Table adapted from http://money.cnn.com/best/bplive/details

1. What is the high temperature in Louisville? _____

2. What is the low temperature in Keller? _____

3. What is the median income per year in the United States? _____

4. Is the median income in Keller higher or lower than the national average? _____

5. How many libraries are within 30 miles of Louisville? _____

6. How many museums are within 30 miles of Keller? _____

7. Where is the personal crime risk higher, in Louisville or Keller? _____

8. Which community has the higher number of colleges? _____

9. Which community has the lower median age? _____

10. In which community is the average commute longer? _____

11. If you are looking for a job, which community is more attractive? _____

12. If you don't want to pay high sales tax, which community is better for you? _____

B Rank the following community features in order of their importance to you.

1 = very important   10 = not important

_____ a strong economy with a lot of jobs

_____ good public schools

_____ low crime

_____ close to colleges and universities

_____ low housing prices

_____ lots of public parks

_____ active community members

_____ a clean environment (no graffiti, litter)

_____ good public transportation

_____ friendly people

_____ good city services, like garbage collection

C Answer the questions about you.

1. Which community in Activity A would you rather live in? Why?

   _____

2. What makes the community you chose more attractive to you?

   _____

3. What are three good features of your city or town?

   _____

4. What are three things that your city or town could improve?

D Complete the sentences with the correct form of a verb from the box.

volunteer   clean up   fight   move   get

1. A group of volunteers is planning _____ the graffiti in our town.

2. The new mayor has promised _____ crime in the city.

3. I'd like _____ at an animal shelter to help abandoned animals.

4. We decided _____ to a city with lower taxes.

5. Many people refuse _____ involved in community issues.

Understanding Community Rules

A These photos show activities and problems at your local park. Complete the flyer with rules. Use *be allowed to, be permitted to, be illegal to,* and *not be allowed to.*

1.

2.

4.

3.

5.

LOS ANGELES COUNTY PARKS & RECREATION
NOTICE TO ALL PARK VISITORS

We are proud of our park. Help to make it more enjoyable. Please observe the following rules:

1. _____
_____

2. _____
_____

3. _____
_____

4. _____
_____

5. _____
_____

B Look at the signs below. Write the rule and give the reason for the rule.

1

3

2

4

RULE	REASON FOR RULE
1. _____ _____	1. _____ _____
2. _____ _____	2. _____ _____
3. _____ _____	3. _____ _____
4. _____ _____	4. _____ _____

Interacting with Police Officers

A Look at Mark Todd's online application for a fishing license.

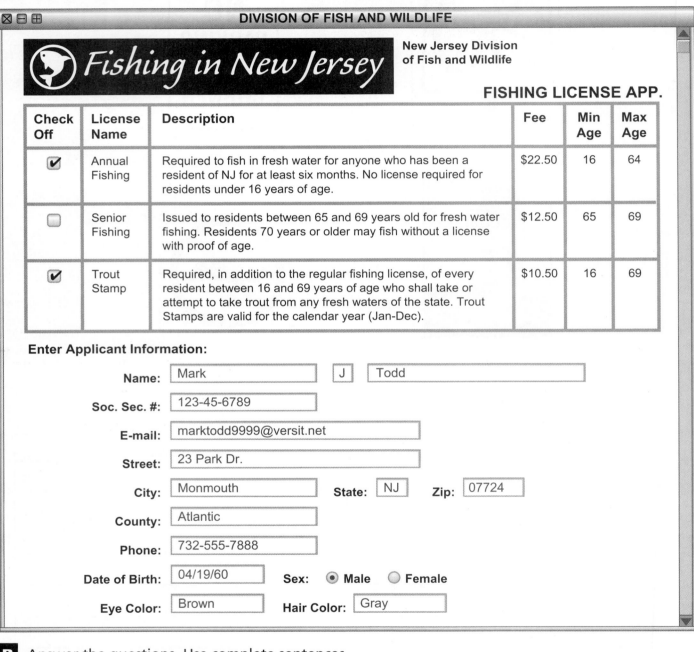

DIVISION OF FISH AND WILDLIFE

Fishing in New Jersey

New Jersey Division of Fish and Wildlife

FISHING LICENSE APP.

Check Off	License Name	Description	Fee	Min Age	Max Age
☑	Annual Fishing	Required to fish in fresh water for anyone who has been a resident of NJ for at least six months. No license required for residents under 16 years of age.	$22.50	16	64
☐	Senior Fishing	Issued to residents between 65 and 69 years old for fresh water fishing. Residents 70 years or older may fish without a license with proof of age.	$12.50	65	69
☑	Trout Stamp	Required, in addition to the regular fishing license, of every resident between 16 and 69 years of age who shall take or attempt to take trout from any fresh waters of the state. Trout Stamps are valid for the calendar year (Jan-Dec).	$10.50	16	69

Enter Applicant Information:

Name: Mark | J | Todd

Soc. Sec. #: 123-45-6789

E-mail: marktodd9999@versit.net

Street: 23 Park Dr.

City: Monmouth   **State:** NJ   **Zip:** 07724

County: Atlantic

Phone: 732-555-7888

Date of Birth: 04/19/60   **Sex:** ● Male ○ Female

Eye Color: Brown   **Hair Color:** Gray

B Answer the questions. Use complete sentences.

1. How old is Mark Todd? _____

2. Can he get a senior fishing license? _____

3. How much will he pay for his fishing license? _____

4. What color is his hair? _____

5. Who needs a trout stamp? _____

C Read the conversation below. Complete the sentences with words from the box.

apologize	apply	license	posted	sign	speeding

Park officer: I need to see your fishing license and some identification, please.

Mark Todd: Here's my driver's _____. Do we need fishing licenses here? I didn't know that.

Park officer: Yes, you do. In fact, it's _____ on the sign at the park entrance.

Mark Todd: I'm sorry, officer. We didn't see the _____. Where can we get a license?

Park officer: You can _____ online or go to the Fish and Game office downtown. I'm afraid you can't fish until you have a license, and I'm going to have to give you a citation.

Mark Todd: Again, I _____. Of course, we won't fish until we get the license.

Park officer: I think you may have also been _____. You can see there's a speed limit for boats coming through this area.

D Complete the sentences about rules in a town park. Use the correct form of the words in parentheses.

1. The park _____ (expect / us / throw away) all our litter.

2. The park _____ (allow / visitors / picnic) in selected areas.

3. The park _____ (warn / us / not park) on the grass.

4. The signs _____ (warn / drivers / not exceed) the speed limits.

5. The park _____ (allow / not / dogs / run) freely.

6. The signs _____ (permit / visitors / fish) in the river.

7. The town _____ (allow / not / park goers / drink) alcoholic beverages.

8. The town _____ (want / us / enjoy) the park.

9. The park _____ (allow / visitors / barbecue) at park barbecue sites.

10. The park _____ (permit / not / people / camp) overnight.

Reporting a Crime

A Read the news articles and complete the chart.

Smokers Get a Break

The City Council passed a new, less-restrictive smoking ordinance yesterday, giving smokers a break.

The new ordinance replaces one passed last year that prohibited smoking in all public buildings. This new ordinance allows smoking in bars and restaurants but prohibits children under 18 years of age from entering without a parent.

Businesses will pay $300 to get permission to allow smoking on the premises. The ordinance takes effect on Sept. 1.

Noise Out, Quiet In

The Town Council voted Tuesday to reduce noise levels within town limits. Beginning June 30, it will be illegal to operate electronic equipment such as radios, CD players, and loudspeakers loud enough to be heard 20 feet away between 10 p.m. and 7 a.m.

In addition, the new ordinance prohibits operating a device if the sound vibration can be felt 20 feet away. This means that drivers cannot play car stereos so loud that it rocks the car next to them at a traffic light.

Violators can be fined up to $2,500 or face 180 days in jail.

Ordinance Limits Dogs and Cats

A new city ordinance that will limit the number of dogs and cats an owner can have takes effect next month. Under the new ordinance, you can have up to four dogs, up to five cats, and no more than six animals total.

Council member Jake Lamont said, "It's just not healthy for the animals or for the people when there are too many pets in a house."

The City Council passed this measure to prevent several problems, including the neglect and mistreatment of animals and unsanitary conditions in neighborhoods.

	Smokers Get a Break	Noise Out, Quiet In	Ordinance Limits Dogs and Cats
What was the problem?			
What does the ordinance allow or prohibit?			
Who passed the law?			
When does it take effect?			

B Reread the articles in Activity A. List two pros (reasons for) and two cons (reasons against) of each law.

	Pros	Cons
Less restrictive smoking ban		
Noise control ordinance		
Pet restrictions		

C Write a paragraph about which ordinance in Activity A you think is best and why.

_____

_____

_____

_____

_____

D Look at the following situations. Should people report these actions to the police?

Situations	Should report	Should not report
1. Parent hitting child	☐	☐
2. Child committing a violent crime	☐	☐
3. Drivers talking on cell phones	☐	☐
4. Children tresspassing	☐	☐
5. Children smoking cigarettes	☐	☐
6. Cars going through red lights	☐	☐
7. People begging for money on the street	☐	☐
8. Young children seeing R-rated movies	☐	☐

E Answer the question.

Which four actions in Activity D should be reported to parents? Write sentences.

_____

_____

_____

_____

Reading: Paraphrasing

A Reread the article. Paraphrase each of the nine sentences.

Exercise Your Right

Next Tuesday we will have an opportunity to exercise one of our most important rights as citizens—the right to vote. As citizens, we not only have the right, we have the duty to vote. This election will determine who will represent us at the local, state and national level. We may need to work or to go to school that day. We might want to avoid the lines at the voting places. We may be frustrated with our political leaders and wish to stay home.

Yes, there are good reasons to stay home on Tuesday, but there are even better reasons to go to the polls. Go early to miss the lines, get a babysitter to take care of the kids, or call your boss to explain you'll be late, but go and vote. It's important to participate in government by voting.

1. *Citizens can use their right to vote in the election next week.*

2. _____

3. _____

4. _____

5. _____

6. _____

7. _____

8. _____

9. _____

B Read the article. Paraphrase each of the six sentences.

NEIGHBORHOOD CRIME WATCH GROUPS

The neighborhood crime watch movement started more than 30 years ago. Through neighborhood crime watch organizations, local officials, law enforcement officers, and members of the community work together to keep a neighborhood safe. This approach has helped reduce problems in high-crime areas. The idea is a simple one—neighbors keep an eye on the neighborhood, reporting any suspicious activity to police. Members of a neighborhood crime watch group do not take action; they just observe and report to authorities.

For information about how to start your own neighborhood crime watch program and for resources to help your group succeed, go to our website.

1. _____

2. _____

3. _____

4. _____

5. _____

6. _____

Writing: Summarizing

A Reread the articles from Lesson 4 and read the summaries. Each summary has a problem. Explain what the problem is.

Smokers Get a Break

The City Council passed a new, less restrictive smoking ordinance yesterday, giving smokers a break.

The new ordinance replaces one passed last year that prohibited smoking in all public places. This new ordinance allows smoking in bars and restaurants but prohibits children under 18 years of age from entering without a parent.

Businesses will pay $300 to get permission to allow smoking on the premises. The ordinance takes effect on Sept. 1.

Summary: Yesterday, the city council voted on a new smoking ordinance. The new ordinance will be harder on smokers. Last year, the city council passed another smoking ordinance, and it said that no one could smoke in public places. The new law begins on Sept. 1.

Problem: _____

_____

Noise Out, Quiet In

The Town Council voted Tuesday to reduce noise levels within town limits. Beginning June 30, it will be illegal to operate electronic equipment such as radios, CD players, and loudspeakers loud enough to be heard 20 feet away between 10 P.M. and 7 A.M.

In addition, the new ordinance prohibits operating a device if the sound vibration can be felt 20 feet away. This means that drivers cannot play car stereos so loud that it rocks the car next to them at a traffic light.

Violators can be fined up to $2,500 or face 180 days in jail.

Summary: The town council passed a new ordinance to prohibit any radios, CD players, or loudspeakers. Also, drivers cannot play car stereos.

Problem: _____

_____

B Reread the article. Write a summary for the article.

> **Ordinance Limits Dogs and Cats**
>
> A new city ordinance that will limit the number of dogs and cats an owner can have takes effect next month. Under the new ordinance, you can have up to four dogs, up to five cats, and no more than six animals total.
>
> Council member Jake Lamont said, "It's just not healthy for the animals or for the people when there are too many pets in a house."
>
> City Council passed this measure to prevent several problems, including the neglect and mistreatment of animals and unsanitary conditions in a neighborhood.

Summary: _____

_____

_____

_____

_____

C Find a news story in your local newspaper or online. Answer the questions.

1. What happened? _____

_____

2. Where? _____

_____

3. Who was involved? _____

_____

4. When did it happen? _____

_____

5. How or why did it happen? _____

_____

D Write a summary of the article you found. Be sure to include your answers from Activity C.

_____

_____

_____

_____

_____

Work: Trash Disposal and Recycling

A Read the text. Then answer the question.

Did you know that about 60% of what you throw away can be recycled? When you recycle something, it is made into something useful. Recycling is an important way to protect our environment. What can you recycle in your city? Each city has different guidelines for recycling, so it is important to know the guidelines for your community. If you aren't sure, go to city hall or check you city's website on the Internet.

What do you usually recycle? _____

_____

B Read the information on recycling. Then, check which items can go into a recycling bin.

City Environmental Services Office

RECYCLING BASICS

CANS & CARTONS
Recycling bin
Beverage cartons and boxes
Tin, aluminum, and steel cans and lids
Food and beverage cans
Not for recycling bin
Foil containers

PAPER & CARDBOARD
Cardboard
Magazines and catalogues
Telephone books
Egg cartons
Newspapers and office paper
Shoe boxes and shopping bags

Not for recycling bin
Paper take-out containers; Pizza boxes

GLASS
Recycling bin
Brown, clear, and green bottles and jars
Food and beverage containers
Not for recycling bin
Drinking glasses, light bulbs, mirrors, windows

PLASTICS
Recycling bin
Juice jugs
Soda, water, mouthwash containers
Detergent bottles
Milk jugs, yogurt and margarine containers
Medicine bottles
Egg cartons

Not for recycling bin
Disposable diapers, plastic bubble wrap, hangers, garden hoses, shoes, toys, utensils. Return plastic bags to grocery stores for recycling.

	Yes	No			Yes	No
1. plastic containers	☐	☐	6. cardboard		☐	☐
2. old note cards	☐	☐	7. pizza boxes		☐	☐
3. light bulbs	☐	☐	8. aluminum cans		☐	☐
4. plastic soap bottles	☐	☐	9. soda bottles		☐	☐
5. plastic shopping bags	☐	☐	10. toys		☐	☐

C Read city information about how to dispose of (throw away) special items. Then read the statements and circle *True* or *False*.

Information for Residents

The city provides trash pickup for all residents. However, the following items cannot be put in the trash.

Household Hazardous Waste

Hazardous materials such as batteries, cleaning fluids, fluorescent light bulbs, paint, lawn and pool chemicals, medical waste, and mercury thermometers cannot be put in the trash. There are Household Hazardous Waste Disposal Days four times a year. Call the County Office at 555-1234 for the next date.

Large Item Collection

You can call the city to pick up large items, such as mattresses, sofas, refrigerators, or tires. There is a small fee. To schedule a pick-up appointment and find out the cost, call 555-5678. Residents of apartments and condos should contact their property managers to arrange a large item pick-up.

Electronics

Electronics such as cell phones, digital cameras, stereos, old electronic products, computers, and televisions must be recycled safely. The city has a monthly E-waste Collection on the first Saturday of every month at City Hall. Residents should bring their e-waste for special recycling.

1.	Batteries cannot be put in the trash because they are hazardous waste.	**True**	**False**
2.	The city will pick up an old stove at your residence for no cost.	**True**	**False**
3.	If you live in an apartment, call the city to schedule a pick-up of a sofa.	**True**	**False**
4.	"E-waste" means electronic products that are no longer useful.	**True**	**False**
5.	E-waste can be recycled with household hazardous waste.	**True**	**False**
6.	There is an e-waste collection day every month.	**True**	**False**
7.	There is a small fee to leave off e-waste at city hall.	**True**	**False**

Family: Child Discipline

A Read the article. Then check *True* or *False*. Correct the false statements.

DISCIPLINING CHILDREN

When you were a child, did your dad or mom spank you when you did something wrong? Nowadays fewer and fewer children get hit on their bottoms as punishment. An increasing number of parents prefer to use forms of discipline other than physical punishment. In fact, punishing your children by hitting them may be considered child abuse in some places. Fortunately, there are many other ways to get your children to behave.

It's important to tell your children what you want in a positive way. For example, "Use words," instead of "Don't hit your brother," tells your child what behavior is expected and reinforces that communication is better than violence.

Parents should also set clear limits. It's impossible to set rules for everything, so you should think about what is most important. Usually parents create rules to prevent people from getting hurt, protect property, and encourage respect for others.

When a child does something wrong, parents should respond appropriately. For example, if your son comes in too late at night, you might make him stay in for the rest of the week. Sometimes just separating the child from the rest of the family or the activity for a little while can be an effective punishment. This is often called giving the child a time out.

1. Today more American parents are spanking their children as punishment than in the past.
   ☐ True   ☐ False

2. According to the article, "Don't fight" is an example of a good rule.
   ☐ True   ☐ False

3. American parents discipline their children the same way as they did 50 years ago.
   ☐ True   ☐ False

4. According to the article, rules about safety are not very important.

   ☐ True   ☐ False

5. One effective punishment is to send the child away from the rest of the family for a few minutes.

   ☐ True   ☐ False

6. It's important to tell children what behavior you expect from them.

   ☐ True   ☐ False

B Answer the questions about you.

1. What is one mistake you made as a child?

   _____

   _____

2. Were you punished for the mistake? If so, how?

   _____

   _____

3. In your culture or family, how are children disciplined when they do something wrong?

   _____

   _____

4. What is one thing that surprises you about how parents discipline children in this country?

   _____

   _____

TAKE IT OUTSIDE: INTERVIEW A FAMILY MEMBER, FRIEND, OR COWORKER. ASK THE QUESTIONS IN ACTIVITY B. TAKE NOTES. WRITE THREE SENTENCES SUMMARIZING THEIR ANSWERS.

_____

_____

_____

_____

_____

_____

Practice Test

DIRECTIONS: Refer to the application form to answer the next five questions. Use the Answer Sheet.

Enter Applicant Information

        First   MI   Last

① Name: _____

② Soc. Sec. #: _____

③ Email: _____

④ Street: _____

City: _____ State: _____ Zip: _____

County: _____

Phone: _____

⑤ Date of Birth: _____ Sex: _____

⑥ Eye color: _____ Hair color: _____

⑦ Check license desired:
- ☐ regular fishing
- ☐ senior
- ☐ child

---

1. On which part of the application would you put your e-mail address?
   A. Part 1
   B. Part 2
   C. Part 7
   D. Part 3

2. Where would you write your eye color?
   A. Part 1
   B. Part 6
   C. Part 4
   D. Part 2

3. What information do you need?
   A. your county
   B. your country
   C. your driver's license number
   D. your occupation

4. How many types of licenses are there?
   A. 1
   B. 2
   C. 3
   D. 4

5. Which part lists your date of birth?
   A. Part 1
   B. Part 3
   C. Part 5
   D. Part 7

ANSWER SHEET

	A	B	C	D
1	Ⓐ	Ⓑ	Ⓒ	Ⓓ
2	Ⓐ	Ⓑ	Ⓒ	Ⓓ
3	Ⓐ	Ⓑ	Ⓒ	Ⓓ
4	Ⓐ	Ⓑ	Ⓒ	Ⓓ
5	Ⓐ	Ⓑ	Ⓒ	Ⓓ
6	Ⓐ	Ⓑ	Ⓒ	Ⓓ
7	Ⓐ	Ⓑ	Ⓒ	Ⓓ
8	Ⓐ	Ⓑ	Ⓒ	Ⓓ
9	Ⓐ	Ⓑ	Ⓒ	Ⓓ
10	Ⓐ	Ⓑ	Ⓒ	Ⓓ

DIRECTIONS: Read the article below to answer the next five questions. Use the Answer Sheet on page 108.

WALK TO HELP MOM CHANGE DOG LAW

A 20–mile fund-raising walk will take place on Saturday to raise money for the mother of a six-year-old boy killed by pit bulls in March. Bobby Taylor was bitten by his neighbor's dogs as he played outside in his yard. Bobby died as a result of the bites. Now his mother, Kim Taylor, is trying to get the City Council to prohibit pit bulls and other dangerous breeds of dog.

Taylor has collected 2,000 signatures for her petition. She is raising funds for flyers, TV ads, and newspaper ads that will explain the law and ask others to help. City Council members will consider the petition next year.

6. What is happening on Saturday?
   A. a walk
   B. a City Council meeting
   C. a new law
   D. a petition

7. Why does Kim Taylor want to prohibit pit bulls?
   A. They're noisy.
   B. They're playful.
   C. They're dangerous.
   D. They're friendly.

8. Who will make the decision about the law?
   A. petition
   B. the City Council
   C. Kim Taylor
   D. neighbors

9. Who is Bobby Taylor?
   A. Kim's brother
   B. Kim's husband
   C. Kim's father
   D. Kim's son

10. When will City Council vote?
   A. on Saturday
   B. in March
   C. next year
   D. tonight

HOW DID YOU DO? Count the number of correct answers on your answer sheet. Record this number in the bar graph on the inside back cover.

Qualities of a Job or Workplace

A Read the article.

WHAT'S THE RIGHT CAREER FOR YOU?

Trying to decide what career is best for you can be difficult. Begin thinking about one now, if you haven't decided yet. Many career counselors use the Holland Code to help students decide on a career. It was developed by Dr. John Holland to describe personality and job types. There are six categories.

Realistic people like to work with their hands, work outside, solve problems, and build or fix things. Firefighting is a realistic career.

Investigative people like working with numbers or science. They are interested in ideas, like to solve problems, and are often good with computers. Scientists and computer programmers are investigative professionals.

Conventional people like detail-oriented and organized workplaces. They may like working with math, finance, and computers. They also like to work with information. Accounting is a conventional occupation.

Artistic people are creative and often prefer being in casual work environments. They like to sing, dance, act, write, and communicate with others. Actors and designers are artistic people.

Enterprising people often like business or politics. They are confident and like to persuade others. They like to speak in public and lead others. Sales and law are enterprising fields.

Social people enjoy helping others and working in the community. They like to talk, and they get along well with others. Teaching and nursing are social careers.

B Complete the sentences with a bold word from the article in Activity A.

1. A police officer is an example of a(n) _____ professional.
2. A tech support specialist is probably a(n) _____ person.
3. A physician assistant is probably a(n) _____ person.
4. An admittance clerk is probably a(n) _____ person.
5. Film producers are usually _____ people.
6. The president is probably a(n) _____ person.

C Look at the photos. Identify the job and write the category from Activity A. Write what you think the person likes about the job.

1.

Job: Category:

Likes: _____

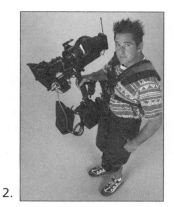

2.

Job: Category:

Likes: _____

3.

Job: Category:

Likes: _____

4.

Job: Category:

Likes: _____

5.

Job: Category:

Likes: _____

6.

Job: Category:

Likes: _____

Understanding Medical Benefits

A Complete the paragraph with the words or phrases in the box. Use each word or phrase only once.

co-pay	deductible	dependents	domestic partners
Network	Open Access	out of pocket	premium

Here at McKay's Department Store, employees can choose from a number of different medical benefits plans. One choice is the _____ Plan.
(1)
With this plan, employees can see the healthcare provider of their choice.
Members of the _____ Plan, however, must choose from a list of
(2)
doctors. Each plan has a different monthly _____. Employees
(3)
may pay $20 a month for one plan and $30 a month for the other. The Open
Access Plan does not have a _____, but with the Network Plan,
(4)
members must pay from $100 to $300 per year before the medical plan begins to
pay for services. The maximum _____ is $1,200 for the Network
(5)
Plan and $1,800 for the Open Access Plan. In other words, you won't pay
more than $1,200 or $1,800 per year, depending on the plan you choose. The Network Plan requires a $20
_____ per doctor's visit, but the Open Access Plan does not require any payment for office visits.
(6)
These plans cover employees' _____ , such as husbands, wives, _____, and children.
(7)   (8)

B Read the choices. Express your preference. Write sentences with *prefer*, *'d prefer*, or *'d rather* (*not*) and the correct form of the verb.

1. work with people / work with machines

   _____

2. have a night shift / have a day shift

   _____

3. be a lab technician / be a medical records specialist

   _____

4. have a high salary / have good benefits

   _____

5. enroll in the Open-Access Plan / enroll in the Network Plan

_____

6. get a job in sales / get a job in product development

_____

C Complete the following conversations. Use the cues in parentheses

1. **Mary Brown:** I'm excited about your offer, but first I'd like to know more about the benefits.

_____? (offer / health care benefits)

   Jane Smith: Yes, we do. We offer a great medical insurance plan with low co-pays for routine visits.

2. **Mary Brown:** _____? (what / family leave policy)

   Jane Smith: Six weeks paid leave and four weeks unpaid.

3. **Mary Brown:** _____? (on-site basic skills courses)

   Jane Smith: Yes, GED and Adult ESL.

4. **Mary Brown:** _____? (provide / tuition reimbursement)

   Jane Smith: No, we don't. The company does offer some on-site training though.

5. **Mary Brown:** _____? (what / other benefits)

   Jane Smith: Other benefits include an on-site gym and on-site day care.

D Write three questions you would ask about benefits during a job interview.

1. _____

2. _____

3. _____

Calling About a Job

A Put the statements in order to make a conversation. Order them 1 to 10.

_____ **Ms. Nevins:** It starts at $30,000, but it depends on experience.

_1_ **Katia:** Hello, I'm calling about the ad for a writer.

_____ **Ms. Nevins:** At least two years at a magazine or newspaper.

_____ **Katia:** What should I do if I want to apply?

_____ **Ms. Nevins:** Yes, how can I help you?

_____ **Katia:** Would you know the salary range?

_____ **Ms. Nevins:** Sure. Go to our website and click on "Contact us" and then "Rose Nevins."

_____ **Katia:** And what kind of experience are you looking for?

_____ **Ms. Nevins:** You can send two copies of your résumé and a cover letter to 1300 South Street, San Pedro, California, 90731, attention Rose Nevins.

_____ **Katia:** Can I send them electronically?

B Answer the questions. Use complete sentences.

1. What position is Katia interested in? _____

_____

2. What is the lowest salary possible? _____

_____

3. How many years of experience are required? _____

_____

4. What are two ways Katia can send her resume? _____

_____

C Unscramble the words to write questions about a job.

1. salary / can / the / you / starting / tell me /

    _____?

2. the name / could / me / of the open position / you / tell /

    _____

    _____?

3. the supervisor's / I / ask / may / name /

    _____?

4. you / the duties / can / me / tell / about

    _____?

5. the qualifications / tell / you / me / could /

    _____?

D Complete the conversation with the correct form of the verb in parentheses. Use present or future forms of *be able to*.

Rob: Hello. I'm calling about the ad for a gardener.

Ms. Mara   Yes. Do you have any experience?

Rob: Yes, I've been a gardener for five years.

Ms. Mara   Good. _____ (work) with all kinds of plants?

Rob: Yes, I have worked with almost everything that grows.

Ms. Mara   And _____ (carry) heavy pots and plants?

Rob: No problem. I am very strong. I _____ (lift) 200 pounds.

Ms. Mara: Good. _____ (drive) a truck?

Rob: I've never driven one before, but I'm sure I can learn.

Ms. Mara: If I have a party, _____ (help out)?

Rob: I'd be happy to.

Ms. Mara: Okay. If you come tomorrow morning, you _____ (start) right away.

Rob: I'll be there.

Reading and Writing a Résumé

A Read the résumé. Then answer the questions.

Eva Wong

3015 Atlantic Avenue
Houston, Texas 70057
713-555-3568 • evawong@global.net

OBJECTIVE

To obtain a job as a Medical Assistant

PROFESSIONAL EXPERIENCE

Miller Hospital

Medical Assistant, 2009–Present

- Interview patients, measure patients' temperature, blood pressure, weight, and height
- Prepare patient examination rooms
- Clean medical instruments
- Schedule appointments, send out bills, and complete insurance forms
- Organize and maintain computerized office and patient records

Houston Central Clinic

Medical Receptionist, 2006–2009

- Managed a computerized front desk for a busy medical office
- Answered calls, maintained medical records, and collected co-payments
- Gave laboratory test results and doctor's instructions to patients

EDUCATION

Houston Community College
A.A.S. degree in Liberal Arts, 2005

---

1. What kind of job does Eva want? _____

2. How can someone contact her? _____

3. How many years work experience does she have? _____

4. Does she have experience working with computers? _____

5. Where did she get her degree? _____

6. What skills does she have? _____

B Complete the application form for Eva Wong. Use the information from Activity A.

Children's Medical Center
Job Application

Name: _____

Address: _____

Telephone No: _____ Email: _____

Position you are applying for: _____

WORK EXPERIENCE: (start with your most recent job)

1. Position: _____ Dates: _____ Company: _____

Duties: _____

_____

_____

C Complete the interview between the hiring manager of the Children's Medical Center and Eva Wong. Use the information from Activity A.

1. **Manager:** So why are you interested in working here at the Children's Medical Center?

   Eva: _____

2. **Manager:** We get a lot of calls every day. How do you feel about working a busy front desk?

   Eva: _____

3. **Manager:** What kind of experience do you have working directly with patients?

   Eva: _____

4. **Manager:** Often our patients have special needs. How flexible are you about trying new things?

   Eva: _____

5. **Manager:** We deal a lot with insurance companies. What experience do you have handling insurance forms?

   Eva: _____

6. **Manager:** Can you tell me about your experience working with computers in an office?

   Eva: _____

Reading: Making Inferences

A Read the paragraph and answer the questions. Write one piece of evidence from the paragraph that supports your answer.

Ben is the owner of a small business in Pittsburgh. His company makes and sells specialty T-shirts. Ben has 10 to 12 employees at any one time. His wife is the bookkeeper, and his son does the marketing. Ben wants to provide his employees with good benefits, but he worries about health insurance. The cost of providing quality health insurance for just a dozen employees is very high, and Ben doesn't know if he can afford it anymore. This issue is very important to Ben. In the next election, he plans to vote for the candidates that he thinks will do the most to make health care manageable.

1. Do you think Ben has a stressful job? _____

   What is the **evidence** for your answer?

   _____

2. Do you think Ben wants to be a good boss? _____

   Evidence: _____

3. Do you think Ben is an American citizen? _____

   Evidence: _____

4. Do you think Ben's family dislikes his job? _____

   Evidence: _____

B Read the job listing. Then read the inference and check *True* or *False*. Write a piece of evidence that supports your answer.

> **Administrative Assistant**
>
> **Duties:** Maintain business and community contacts, help director with meetings, schedule appointments and interviews, assist with the budget.
> **Qualifications:** Four years of experience in office setting, preferably in the media, excellent computer skills, can deal with the public in a professional manner, ability to handle stress, college degree preferred.

1. The administrative assistant should be good with numbers.   ☐ True   ☐ False

   Evidence:_____

2. You won't have to use the computer in this position.   ☐ True   ☐ False

   Evidence:_____

3. This position is probably relaxing.   ☐ True   ☐ False

   Evidence:_____

4. The administrative assistant needs to be good with people.   ☐ True   ☐ False

   Evidence:_____

5. This position is probably in television or at a magazine or newspaper.   ☐ True   ☐ False

   Evidence:_____

C Read the letter. Then, answer the questions with complete sentences.

Dear Human Resources Director:

I am writing in response to your ad for an account assistant in the *Los Angeles Times* on May 3. I would enjoy the opportunity to meet with you to discuss this position.

As you can see in the enclosed résumé, I have worked in sales and marketing for three years since I graduated from the University of Southern California. I have excellent computer and communication skills. I am able to deal with pressure, meet deadlines, and manage multiple responsibilities at one time.

Sincerely,
Rebecca Andersson

1. Do you think the writer is organized? Why or why not? _____

   _____

2. What duties do you think the account assistant might have? Why?

   _____

   _____

3. What qualities do you think the writer might have that are not mentioned?

   _____

   _____

4. What question might the interviewer ask Rebecca?

   _____

   _____

Writing: Writing and Revising a Cover Letter

A Read the cover letter. Find and correct 10 errors in grammar and punctuation. Then, find and underline 3 other errors in content.

89 parker St
South Gate, CA 90280

May 16, 2012

Linda hooper
Director
Excite marketing
445 Broad Ave
Rowland Heights, CA 91748

Dear Mx. Hooper:

   I write inresponse to your ad for an administrative assistant in the *LA Daily News* on May 11. I would will enjoy the opportunity to meet you to speak about this position.

   As you can see in the enclosed résumé, I work as an office clerk for three years. I started when I was in high school. My father moved here from Michigan (he got a better job). I am very organized and I like to work with people. I have good computer skills. My mother says I have a nice phone voice, too. Even though I'm only twenty, I am a hard worker.

   I am very interested in the position of administrative assistant at Excited Marketing. I would appreciate the opportunity to discus my qualifications in person.

Sincerely

Katie Grant

B Read the letter in Activity A. List three things in the letter that don't need to be included.

1. _____

2. _____

3. _____

C Rewrite the second paragraph of the letter in Activity A and include only the relevant information.

_____

_____

_____

_____

_____

D Look at the template below. On a separate piece of paper, write a cover letter for a job.

Your name
Your address
Your phone number

Date

Recipient's Name
Recipient's Job
Recipient's Address

Dear _____:

Write about the job you want to apply for, how you heard about the job, and when you heard about the job.

Highlight important information on your résumé that shows you can do the job you are applying for.

Thank the recipients for their attention and say when you will contact them for an interiew.

Sincerely,

Sign your name

Type your name

Family: Family and Medical Leave

A Read the information about the Family and Medical Leave Act (FMLA). This law allows employees to take leave for serious medical problems.

Family and Medical Leave Act (FMLA)
Frequently Asked Questions and Answers

Q: *How much leave am I entitled to under FMLA?*
A: If you are an "eligible" employee, you are entitled to 12 weeks of leave for certain family and medical reasons during a 12-month period.

Q: *Which employees are eligible to take FMLA leave?*
A: Employees are eligible to take FMLA leave if they have worked for their employer for at least 12 months, and have worked for at least 1,250 hours over the previous 12 months, and work at a location where at least 50 employees are employed by the employer within 75 miles.

Q: *Does the law guarantee paid time off?*
A: No. The FMLA only requires unpaid leave. However, the law permits an employee to elect to, or the employer to require the employee to use accrued paid leave, such as vacation or sick leave, for some or all of the FMLA leave period. When paid leave is substituted for unpaid FMLA leave, it may be counted against the 12-week FMLA leave entitlement if the employee is properly notified of the designation when the leave begins.

Q: *Can the employer count leave taken due to pregnancy complications against the 12 weeks of FMLA leave for the birth and care of my child?*
A: Yes. An eligible employee is entitled to a total of 12 weeks of FMLA leave in a 12-month period. If the employee has to use some of that leave for another reason, including a difficult pregnancy, it may be counted as part of the 12-week FMLA leave entitlement.

Q: *Who is considered an immediate "family member" for purposes of taking FMLA leave?*
A: An employee's spouse, children (son or daughter), and parents are immediate family members for purposes of FMLA. The term "parent" does not include a parent "in-law." The terms *son* or *daughter* do not include individuals age 18 or over unless they are "incapable of self-care" because of mental or physical disability that limits one or more of their "major life activities" as those terms are defined in regulations issued by the Equal Employment Opportunity Comission (EEOC) under the Americans With Disabilities Act (ADA).

Source: http://www.dol.gov/elaws/esa/fmla/faq.asp

B Answer the questions.

1. How much time off can you get for family or medical leave? _____

2. Does your employer have to pay you for this time? _____

3. Do adult children usually count as immediate family? _____

4. Can you use sick leave instead of FMLA leave? _____

5. Which employees are guaranteed FMLA leave? _____

C Answer the questions.

1. How many days were you sick last year? _____

2. How many days did you miss work or school because you were sick? _____

3. How many days did you take care of someone else who was sick? _____

4. Does anyone in your household have a serious medical problem? If yes, who takes care of him or her?

   _____

TAKE IT OUTSIDE: INTERVIEW A FAMILY MEMBER, FRIEND, OR COWORKER. WRITE THEIR ANSWERS.

1. What work benefit do you think is the most helpful to an employee with a family?

   _____

   _____

2. Which benefits, if any, do you get from your job that help your family?

   _____

   _____

3. If you could change one thing about your job to help your family life, what would it be?

   _____

   _____

Work: Employment Discrimination

A Read the government information on employment discrimination (Title VII).

⊠ ⊟ ⊞   **FEDERAL EQUAL EMPLOYMENT OPPORTUNITY LAWS**

The U.S. Equal Employment Opportunity Commission

FEDERAL EQUAL EMPLOYMENT OPPORTUNITY LAWS (EEOC)

Under federal laws, it is illegal to discriminate in any aspect of employment, including:
- hiring and firing;
- compensation, assignment, or classification of employees;
- transfer, promotion, layoff, or recall;
- job advertisements;
- recruitment;
- testing;
- use of company facilities;
- training and apprenticeship programs;
- fringe benefits;
- pay, retirement plans, and disability leave; or
- other terms and conditions of employment.

Discriminatory practices under these laws also include:
- harassment on the basis of race, color, religion, sex, national origin, disability, or age;
- retaliation against an individual for filing a charge of discrimination, participating in an investigation, or opposing discriminatory practices;
- employment decisions based on stereotypes or assumptions about the abilities, traits, or performance of individuals of a certain sex, race, age, religion, or ethnic group, or individuals with disabilities; and
- denying employment opportunities to a person because of marriage to, or association with, an individual of a particular race, religion, national origin, or an individual with a disability. Title VII also prohibits discrimination because of participation in schools or places of worship associated with a particular racial, ethnic, or religious group.

Employers are required to post notices to all employees advising them of their rights under the laws EEOC enforces and their right to be free from retaliation. Such notices must be accessible, as needed, to persons with visual or other disabilities that affect reading.

Source: http://www.eeoc.gov/facts/qanda.html

B Check *True* or *False*. Use the information in Activity A.

1. An employer can refuse to hire you if you are not qualified.
   ☐ True   ☐ False

2. An employer can fire you if you join a new religion.
   ☐ True   ☐ False

3. Under federal law you cannot be fired because you are too old.
   ☐ True   ☐ False

4. It's okay for employers to treat you differently because English is not your first language.
   ☐ True   ☐ False

5. An employer can fire an employee for reporting discrimination.
   ☐ True   ☐ False

6. An employer can let you go if you are disorganized at work.
   ☐ True   ☐ False

7. An employer must inform employees of their rights.
   ☐ True   ☐ False

TAKE IT OUTSIDE: INTERVIEW A FAMILY MEMBER, FRIEND, OR COWORKER. WRITE THEIR ANSWERS.

1. Has anyone ever treated you unfairly because of your national origin, race, religion, or gender? If so, how?

   _____

2. In your workplace, do men and women hold the same jobs?

   _____

3. Do you think employment practices in this country are generally fair?

   _____

4. What advice would you give to someone who is looking for work in this country for the first time?

   _____

Practice Test

DIRECTIONS: Refer to the job application form to answer the next five questions. Use the Answer Sheet.

Carter Company
Lynwood, CA

Job Application Form
(PLEASE PRINT)

(1) Name: _Daniel Gomez_

Address: _1655 Maple Street, El Monte, CA 91731_

(2) Telephone No: _626-555-8822_   email: _ddgogomez@global.net_

Position you are applying for: _Accountant_

(3) **WORK EXPERIENCE:** (start with your most recent job)

1. Position: _____ Dates: _____ Company: _____

Duties: _____

_____

(4) 2. Position: _____ Dates: _____ Company: _____

Duties: _____

_____

(5) **EDUCATION:**

School	Dates attended	Graduated	Degree

1. On what part of the application would you list your most recent job?
   A. Part 1   B. Part 2   C. Part 3   D. Part 4

2. Where would you say what job you are applying for?
   A. Part 1   B. Part 2   C. Part 3   D. Part 4

3. Where would you list the schools you attended?
   A. Part 5   B. Part 4   C. Part 3   D. Part 2

4. Who is the applicant?
   A. accountant   B. Daniel Gomez   C. Carter Company   D. ddgogomez

5. Who is the employer?
   A. accountant   B. Daniel Gomez   C. Carter Company   D. ddgogomez

ANSWER SHEET

	A	B	C	D
1	A	B	C	D
2	A	B	C	D
3	A	B	C	D
4	A	B	C	D
5	A	B	C	D
6	A	B	C	D
7	A	B	C	D
8	A	B	C	D
9	A	B	C	D
10	A	B	C	D

DIRECTIONS: Read the job listings to answer the next five questions. Use the Answer Sheet on page 126.

New Listings:

KBNC, Pomona, CA
WRITER
Duties: Will write news stories, write live updates, contact sources by phone, help producer develop graphics.
Qualifications: College degree preferred. News writing experience preferred. Excellent writing skills, good command of English, attentive to details, good computer skills, ability to gather information quickly, ability to work on a team and meet deadlines.

KNRR, Hollywood, CA
PRODUCTION ASSISTANT
Duties: Write, help producer, schedule guests for shows, research story ideas.
Qualifications: College degree, excellent writing skills, good organizational skills, creative, strong computer skills. Must have excellent communication skills and be able to deal with pressure.

KQAP, Burbank, CA
ACCOUNT ASSISTANT
Duties: Sell advertising time to advertising agencies and retail businesses. Call on community contacts to develop new business. Develop and maintain business contacts.
Qualifications: Minimum three years of sales experience preferred. Ability to meet goals. Excellent oral and written communication skills, strong mathematical ability, California driver's license and personal transportation required.

KUPS, Paramount, CA
CAMERA OPERATOR
Duties: Operate camera at the station and on location with news teams.
Qualifications: Minimum two years of experience.

6. Which job requires a driver's license?
   A. writer
   B. production assistant
   C. account assistant
   D. camera operator

7. Which job is in Hollywood?
   A. writer
   B. production assistant
   C. account assistant
   D. camera operator

8. Which job requires two years of experience?
   A. writer
   B. production assistant
   C. account assistant
   D. camera operator

9. Where is the writing job?
   A. Hollywood
   B. Burbank
   C. Paramount
   D. Pomona

10. What is a duty of the account assistant?
    A. operate a camera
    B. schedule guests
    C. develop graphics
    D. call on businesses

HOW DID YOU DO? Count the number of correct answers on your answer sheet. Record this number in the bar graph on the inside back cover.

Identifying Ways People Communicate

A Look at the body language in the photos. Match the photos to the descriptions below.

A

B

C

D

E

F

1. _____ He is not telling the truth.

2. _____ He is expressing his approval to someone.

3. _____ He is showing everybody that he won.

4. _____ She doesn't know something.

5. _____ She is going to ask a question.

6. _____ She is asking someone to be quiet.

B Write sentences about what you think each person is doing.

A. *She is shrugging because her teacher asked her what happened to her homework.*

B. _____

C. _____

D. _____

E. _____

F. _____

C Answer the questions about yourself.

1. What are three ways that you communicate with your friends and family?
   _____

2. Who are the three people you talk to most?
   _____

3. What is one way you communicate today that you didn't use ten years ago?
   _____

4. What is one way you will communicate in ten years that you don't use now?
   _____

D Complete the conversation. Use one of the indefinite pronouns in the box.

| anyone | anything | everyone | no one | nothing | someone | something |

A: Can I help you?

B: Yes, I'm looking for _____ for my brother. It's his birthday tomorrow.

A: Do you have _____ in mind?

B: No, _____ in particular. Can you recommend _____ for _____ who likes electronic gadgets?

A: Yes! This tiny cell phone is the gift that _____ is asking for this year. It's the best on the market.

B: Yes, but I need _____ a little less expensive.

A: Okay. How about this mini MP3 player? You can't get _____ as nice for this price.

B: Hmm. Are you sure _____ else will get him this?

A: It just came in yesterday, so I think you'll be safe.

129

Improving Communication Skills

A Match each remark with one of the communication skills in the box. Write the communication skill on the line.

asking for feedback	complimenting	making a request
asking for help	expressing appreciation	making a suggestion
asking for an opinion	interrupting	offering help

1. Excuse me. I hate to disturb you. _____
2. Am I doing this correctly? _____
3. Can you help me lift this? _____
4. Thanks so much. I was having trouble. _____
5. Sorry to bother you. Got a minute? _____
6. May I help? _____
7. Could you turn down the music? _____
8. Good work. _____
9. How do you like the new office? _____
10. You could call ahead for reservations. _____

B Circle the most appropriate (polite) response.

1. Why don't you put the box over there?

   A. No way.
   B. Thanks for the suggestion, but . . .

2. Great job. That looks really nice.

   A. You're right.
   B. Do you think so? Thanks.

3. I am so sorry. I didn't see you.

   A. That's okay. Don't worry.
   B. Watch out next time.

4. Is there anything that isn't clear?

   A. Yes. The whole thing.
   B. Sorry, could you go over it again?

5. Could you help Marie on the project?

   A. No, I don't like her.
   B. I'd like to, but I'm really busy.

C Look at one of the responses you didn't choose in Activity B. Write the response and explain why it is not appropriate.

_____

_____

_____

_____

D Read the emails below. What is the purpose of each email?

doctor's appoint...
Reply   Reply All   Print   Inbox

From: Lisa@undercover.net
Date: Thursday, May 5, 2012 3:05 PM
To: Annhood@undercover.net
Subject: doctor's appointment

Ann,

I have a doctor's appointment tomorrow afternoon. Could you take my lunch shift? I'd be happy to work your dinner shift.
Let me know.

Thanks,
Lisa

presentation
Reply   Reply All   Print   Inbox

From: Beth Nixon
Date: Tuesday, May 17, 2012 8:05 AM
To: Matt Carpenter
Subject: presentation

Matt,

Thanks again for your great work on the presentation yesterday. I think it went very well. I'm sure we'll get some new business from it.

Beth Nixon

Purpose: _____   Purpose: _____

E You were supposed to meet your daughter's teacher yesterday at 3:00. Unfortunately, you had to work late and you did not have the school's phone number with you. Write a note to the teacher expressing your regret.

_____

_____

_____

_____

_____

Communicating in Different Situations

A Complete the conversation with the responses from the box.

- I might. If I do, I'll ask. Thanks.
- Yes?
- Oh, I'm sorry. Could you tell me what's wrong with it?
- Sure. What is it?
- I guess I was so worried about getting it done on time, I wasn't very careful.

Supervisor: Could I interrupt you for a minute, Sam?

Sam: _____

Supervisor: I'd like to talk to you about this report.

Sam: _____

Supervisor: Well, the thing is, it's not done very well.

Sam: _____

Supervisor: I don't think the numbers in this chart are correct, and there are a lot of spelling and grammar mistakes.

Sam: _____

Supervisor: I understand. If you need more time or more help, you should ask for it. Would you please redo the report? Do you need help rewriting it?

Sam: _____

B Answer the questions about the conversation in Activity A.

1. Who interrupts? _____

2. Who gives feedback? _____

3. Who asks for feedback? _____

4. Who expresses regret? _____

5. Who offers help? _____

6. Who expresses appreciation? _____

C Read the situation. Then re-write each statement using *may* (*not*) or *might* (*not*).

1. Yulin is scratching her head. Perhaps she is worried.

   Yulin is scratching her head. She might be worried.

2. Now Yulin is frowning at her test paper. Maybe she doesn't understand

   _____

3. Perhaps Yulin will ask the teacher for help.

   _____

4. It's possible that the teacher doesn't notice her.

   _____

5. It's possible that Yulin is afraid to interrupt the teacher.

   _____

D Write a conclusion for each situation. Use *must be* or *must not be*.

1. Steve and Mei just got married.

   They must be happy.

2. The teacher is giving back the tests and does not look happy.

   _____

3. Toni goes jogging every day.

   _____

4. The new student always says *please* and *thank* you.

   _____

5. George just got an email and is smiling.

   _____

6. Tina just won the lottery.

   _____

Becoming a Better Listener

A Answer the questions using complete sentences.

1. What are some differences in communication between your culture and American culture? _____

   _____

2. Have you ever had a problem communicating because of a cultural difference? What was the problem and

   why do you think it happened? _____

   _____

B Read the article.

In today's global business world, the ability to communicate across different cultures is very important. Whether it's at work, at school, or in your community, chances are you will come into contact with people from another culture. Here are some tips to make your cross-cultural communication more successful:

- Look for what you have in common with people from another culture rather than what separates you from them. No matter what culture another person comes from, you must have more similarities than differences.

- Share information about your culture and ask about theirs. Remember that your customs are probably a little different. When there is a communication problem, it might be because of a cultural difference.

- Although the people from a culture may be similar in a lot of ways, they are not all the same. Remember you are communicating with one person, not with the entire group.

- When you have a disagreement with someone from another culture, offer any criticism in private. Public criticism may be very embarrassing. Treat the other person as an equal, not as someone below you. Also, be patient. Resolving disagreements can be time-consuming.

C Read the inferences from the article in Activity B. Check *True* or *False*. Then write a piece of evidence from the reading that supports your answer.

1. Nowadays people have to communicate with different cultures.

   ☐ True ☐ False

   Evidence: _____

   _____

   _____

2. In talking to someone from another culture, you should remember that there are communication differences.

   ☐ True ☐ False

   Evidence: _____

   _____

   _____

3. People from the same culture always communicate the same way.

   ☐ True ☐ False

   Evidence: _____

   _____

   _____

4. If you have a problem with someone from another culture, it's best to try to forget about it.

   ☐ True ☐ False

   Evidence: _____

   _____

   _____

D Answer the following questions about vocabulary in the article in Activity B.

1. What expression means the same as *meet*? _____

2. What word means the same as *suggestions*? _____

3. What word means the same as *whole*? _____

4. What word means the same as *solving*? _____

Reading: Fact or Opinion?

A Read the letters. Write two facts and two opinions stated in the letters.

The Herald Forum

In response to "Council Member Parker backs more money for schools" (Sept. 15):

Parker Right to Support Schools
Thank you, Diana Parker, for your support of schools. The extra money could be used to keep our good teachers. My teacher last year quit teaching because the pay was so low and the job was so difficult.

Our school doesn't have a music program anymore because we don't have the money, and we only have art once a week. I want to study music in college, but I won't be able to if I don't begin now.
Lydia Moore

Grant Has My Interests at Heart
Diana Parker, once again, wants to use taxpayers' hard-earned money to promote unnecessary programs in schools. Students need to spend more time on core subjects such as English and math. Music and art just take time away from the important subjects.

Paul Grant has my interests at heart when he opposes Parker's plan. He speaks for the taxpayer, the hardworking members of the community who would rather keep taxes low and spend public money only on essentials.
Don Lee

Fact 1: _____

Fact 2: _____

Opinion 1: _____

Opinion 2: _____

B Read the paragraph and complete the chart.

On February 1, the board voted overwhelmingly to approve a 4% pay raise for all employees. As department head, I thought the board members' decision showed excellent judgment. Without the pay raises, I believe we would have trouble keeping the wonderful teaching staff we currently have. Starting July 15, all employees will receive the 4% raise. Employees who meet certain requirements, such as superior evaluations and at least 5 years employment, will receive an additional 1%. Any questions should be directed to Human Resources.

Facts	Opinions
1. _____ _____	1. _____ _____
2. _____ _____	2. _____ _____

C Read the statements below. Identify one fact and one opinion in each.

1. "In my country, Peru, men touch more often than American men do. I think it's very strange that men here don't touch."

   Fact: _____

   Opinion: _____

2. "Students in most Asian countries are used to the teacher giving lectures. It's a better way to learn."

   Fact: _____

   Opinion: _____

3. "Kissing people on the cheek is a strange way to greet people. It's more common in Europe than it is in the United States."

   Fact: _____

   Opinion: _____

4. "It's very disrespectful when people don't maintain eye contact. My coworker doesn't look me in the eye very often.

   Fact: _____

   Opinion: _____

Writing: Supporting Your Ideas

A Read the following statements and write *Agree* or *Disagree* to express your opinion.

1. Parents should know all of their children's friends. _____

2. Community members need to know each other. _____

3. It's more important to spend time with your family than to make money. _____

4. Workers should never talk back to their supervisors. _____

5. It's not always a good idea to express your anger openly. _____

6. People communicate differently in the United States than they do in my country. _____

B Choose one of the statements from Activity A. Write your opinion about it in the box. Then brainstorm ideas that support your opinion. Write your ideas in the small boxes.

Opinion:

C Choose your two strongest ideas for support from Activity B. Write them in the boxes below. Then write down examples, facts, or personal stories to support and strengthen your ideas.

D Write a paragraph giving your opinion. Use your notes from Activity C to support your opinion.

_____

_____

_____

_____

_____

_____

_____

_____

_____

_____

_____

_____

_____

_____

_____

_____

E Reread your writing. How do you support your opinion? Do you use facts, examples, or personal stories? Do you use more than one kind of support? Which support do you think is the most convincing?

_____

_____

_____

Work: Performance Evaluations

A Read the information about performance evaluations and answer the questions. Use complete sentences.

PERFORMANCE EVALUATIONS

1. Performance evaluations should take place once a year. Supervisors should evaluate employees after giving notice, and then conduct announced observations. Employees will also have the opportunity to provide upward evaluations, that is, to answer questionnaires about their supervisor's performance.

2. After observations, supervisors will complete the evaluation form and then schedule a face-to-face interview with each employee. In the interview, the supervisor will give the employee a copy of the form and explain the evaluation. The employee may ask questions at that time or schedule another time to ask questions about the evaluation.

3. All evaluations (employee and upward) should follow certain guidelines. Comments should be specific and focus on facts, not opinions. For example, "Janice did not turn her quarterly report in on 10/19 as requested," is more specific than "Janice is often disorganized and late with assignments." Comments should relate to workplace behaviors, not personality ("My supervisor is mean and difficult"). Comments should not be general or ambiguous ("Ron might want to work a little harder at some things").

4. If an employee still disagrees with the evaluation after discussion with the supervisor, he or she can submit an appeal in writing. The appeal should state the reasons for the disagreement and provide facts to support the position. Call the Human Resources Office for more information.

1. How often do supervisors evaluate employees? _____

2. What do supervisors have to do before an evaluation? _____

3. What do supervisors do after completing the evaluation form? _____

_____

4. What can employees do if they think the evaluation is wrong? _____

B Answer the following questions about vocabulary in the article in Activity A.

1. In paragraph 1, what phrase means the same as *warning*? _____

2. In paragraph 3, what phrase means the same as *be about*? _____

3. In paragraph 4, what word means the same as *turn in*? _____

C Read the pairs of sentences. Circle the letter of the sentence that follows the guidelines given in Activity A. Then give a reason for your answer.

1. A. "Mr. Peters is lazy and messy."

   B. "Mr. Peters left his tools lying out in his workspace on 12/16."

   Reason: _____

   _____

2. A. "Hannah answers the phone politely and asks visitors to have a seat."

   B. "Hannah is funny and enjoyable to be around."

   Reason: _____

   _____

3. A. "Sonya's work is careless."

   B. "Sonya needs to complete her weekly reports more carefully so she doesn't make errors in calculations."

   Reason: _____

   _____

Family: Communicating with School Personnel

A Read the information. Answer the questions.

Communication with the School

Information. Most schools have several different ways of providing information to students and their families, including materials sent home, website information, and online and printed newsletters and other publications. If you or someone in your family is enrolled in a school, pay attention to any emails you receive or mail that is sent to your home. If you are not receiving information, call the school to find out how you can access information on a regular basis. Take responsibility for being informed.

Participation. Be actively involved in school events. The more you participate in meetings, festivals, and other activities, the more you will feel as if you are part of a community. You will also know more about what's going on at the school and be able to communicate with teachers and other school personnel on a slightly more informal basis. But don't take the opportunity to have a private conversation with a teacher at a public event— schedule an appointment to talk about anything confidential.

Attitude. When you talk to a teacher, whether your own or your child's, remember that you are both professionals. The teacher is a professional educator who should want the best for his or her students. You are a consumer, and being a student is part of your professional development. Don't be afraid to express opinions and needs, but do so in a polite and respectful way. Speak with the teacher as you would a coworker. You both have opinions and may see situations differently, but you both have the right to express those opinions respectfully.

1. List three or more ways a school can provide information to students and parents.

   _____

   _____

   _____

2. List two reasons why you should participate in school events.

   _____

   _____

3. Describe how you should talk to a teacher (yours or your child's).

   _____

   _____

B Read each sentence. Then check if you think it is a good or bad way to express yourself and give your reasons.

Comment to a teacher	Good	Bad	Reason for your opinion
1. At a parent-teacher conference: "Well, you know best. You're the teacher."			
2. At a parent-teacher conference: "I really appreciate how you are helping Katia. Do you know that her grandmother just died?"			
3. At a class party: "I'm very worried about Eric's grades. How can he improve?"			
4. On the telephone to the school: "I'd like to set up an appointment to meet with you and talk about some concerns."			
5. To the teacher in an email: "Can you email me every week to let me know what is happening in school?"			

C Match Mr. Anderson's responses to Sanaz's statements. Then, replace the underlined words with your own ideas and role play. Use the Communication Strategy.

Sanaz	Mr. Anderson
_____ 1. Hello. Is this <u>Mr. Anderson</u>?	a. You're welcome.
_____ 2. Hi, <u>Mr. Anderson</u>. This is <u>Sanaz Miller</u>. I'm in your <u>ESL 3</u> class.	b. I'm sorry to hear that. I hope you feel better soon.
_____ 3. Not so good, really. <u>I've got some kind of infection</u>. I'm afraid I can't come to class tomorrow.	c. Hi, <u>Sanaz</u>. How are you?
_____ 4. Me, too. I'm <u>taking antibiotics</u>, so I should be back on Thursday.	d. Sure. Why don't you send me an email to remind me?
_____ 5. <u>Can you</u> email me the assignments until I get back?	e. Yes, it is.
_____ 6. Thank you so much.	f. That's fine.

COMMUNICATION STRATEGY

Asking Favors Politely

When you ask someone a favor, you are asking that person to do something special for you. It is best to ask very politely, especially when the person is a teacher or a boss.

Can you (email me) ...? Could you (email me) ...?

Would you mind (emailing me) ...? Is it possible for you to (email me) ...?

Practice Test

DIRECTIONS: Read the information about cell phone etiquette to answer the next 5 questions. Use the Answer Sheet.

Cell Phone Etiquette

Do you like listening to other people's conversations on the bus or in the supermarket? Do you like hearing cell phones ringing in the movie theater or the library? If you are like most people, you find this kind of cell phone behavior rude. To help create a more polite society, follow these five rules of cell phone etiquette.

1. Put your cell phone on vibrate in restaurants, public restrooms, buses, subways and other public places. If you receive an important call, go outside to return the call. In movie theaters, libraries, museums, or work meetings, turn your phone off.

2. When people are around, speak quietly and stand 10 feet away.

3. Keep public conversations short.

4. Don't ignore the person you're with. It's rude to answer a cell phone call on a date or when you're out with friends. Let the call go to voice mail and return it later.

5. Talking on the phone while driving is dangerous and against the law in many states. Never do it!

1. Which rule does speaking loudly on a cell phone break?
   A. 1
   B. 2
   C. 3
   D. 4

2. What should you do if you receive an important call in a restaurant?
   A. Ignore it.
   B. Call back immediately.
   C. Go outside to return the call.
   D. Answer it.

3. In which situation is it OK to answer a cell phone call?
   A. In your boss' office.
   B. In a library.
   C. At lunch with a friend.
   D. On the street.

4. Which rule does talking on a cell phone in an elevator break?
   A. 1
   B. 3
   C. 4
   D. 5

5. Which statement is true according to the reading?
   A. Most people have good cell phone etiquette.
   B. It's a good idea to use voicemail.
   C. You should never use a cell phone when you are driving.
   D. It's okay to shout on a cell phone.

ANSWER SHEET

	A	B	C	D
1	A	B	C	D
2	A	B	C	D
3	A	B	C	D
4	A	B	C	D
5	A	B	C	D
6	A	B	C	D
7	A	B	C	D
8	A	B	C	D
9	A	B	C	D
10	A	B	C	D

DIRECTIONS: Refer to the email below to answer the next five questions. Use the Answer Sheet on page 144.

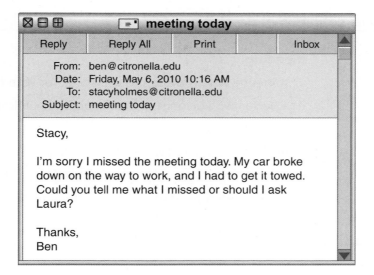

6. Who wrote the message?
   A. Stacy
   B. Ben
   C. Citronella
   D. Laura

7. What is the subject of the email?
   A. meeting today
   B. the car
   C. a tow truck
   D. work

8. What is the purpose of the email?
   A. to criticize
   B. to express appreciation
   C. to check for understanding
   D. to express regret

9. What does the writer NOT do?
   A. express regret
   B. make a request
   C. ask for feedback
   D. express appreciation

10. Who did Ben have a meeting with?
   A. Laura
   B. Stacy
   C. Laura and Stacy
   D. his supervisor

HOW DID YOU DO? Count the number of correct answers on your answer sheet. Record this number in the bar graph on the inside back cover.

The Functions of Government

A Match each word with its definition or description.

Word	Meaning
_____ 1. a bill	a. someone who is chosen to act, speak, or vote for someone else
_____ 2. Congress	b. a person who belongs to the Republican political party
_____ 3. a Democrat	c. a proposal for a law
_____ 4. the press	d. newspapers, radio, TV, and other organizations that present the news
_____ 5. a representative	e. a person who belongs to the Democratic political party
_____ 6. a Republican	f. the elected representatives who help make national laws

B Answer the questions about Congress. Use complete sentences.

1. What are the two groups of Congress?

   _____

2. How many people are in each group of Congress?

   _____

3. What is the job of Congress?

   _____

4. Who is the leader of the Senate?

   _____

5. Who is the leader of the House of Representatives?

   _____

6. Who can be present during meetings of Congress?

   _____

7. What does the press do?

   _____

C Think of a law that you would like to suggest to Congress. Answer the questions. Use complete sentences.

1. What law would you like to suggest?

   _____

2. Why do you think we need this law?

   _____

3. Who would this law affect?

   _____

4. How would this law improve the current situation?

   _____

5. What negative effects might this law have?

   _____

6. Who might disagree with this law? Why?

   _____

D Rewrite the sentences. Replace the underlined words with a phrasal verb from the box. Use the correct form.

count on	hand out	look forward to	run for
find out	get on	run into	show up

1. The representative <u>gave</u> copies of the bill to all members of Congress.

   _____

2. The senator told the members of Congress he <u>was expecting</u> their vote.

   _____

3. Keiko is <u>excited about</u> visiting the White House.

   _____

4. She needs to <u>discover</u> the best way to get to the White House.

   _____

5. She hopes that the President will <u>appear</u> when she is there.

   _____

6. Your brother should <u>campaign for</u> city council. He has good ideas and strong opinions.

   _____

The Branches of Government

A Check *True* or *False* for each statement. There are six false statements.

	True	False
1. The three branches of the U.S. government are the legislative, the executive, and the Constitution.	☐	☐
2. The president is a member of the executive branch of government.	☐	☐
3. The legislative branch proposes bills.	☐	☐
4. The legislative branch must give a bill to the judicial branch before it can become law.	☐	☐
5. The executive branch decides whether proposed laws are constitutional.	☐	☐
6. The judicial branch can veto a bill.	☐	☐
7. The Constitution explains how the government works.	☐	☐
8. *Veto* means to pass a bill.	☐	☐
9. If a law is not considered constitutional, it is not passed.	☐	☐
10. The Supreme Court is part of the legislative branch.	☐	☐

B Rewrite each false statement from Activity A.

1. _____

   _____

2. _____

   _____

3. _____

   _____

4. _____

   _____

5. _____

   _____

6. _____

   _____

C Complete the news report with the words from the box.

bill	House	pass	president
proposed	Senate	unconstitutional	vetoed

This morning, the president _____ a bill that would provide free school supplies to all school
①

students. He explained that due to budget cuts, the government could not afford to pass such a bill at this

time. In related news, the legislative branch has _____ a "Mandatory Health Insurance"
②

_____. If it passes, all citizens will be required either to have health insurance provided by their
③

employers or to pay for their own health insurance. Currently, a large percentage of the population does not

have health insurance. Many here in Washington believe that the Supreme Court will find this bill

_____. The _____ and _____ are not expected to
④   ⑤   ⑥

_____ the bill, but if they do, the _____ will, of course, have to approve it too.
⑦   ⑧

D Rewrite the rules. Complete the sentences with *must, must not, have to,* or *don't have to* and a
verb that keeps the meaning of the rule.

1. Smoking is not allowed in the building. You _____ here.

2. Register to vote before the election. You _____ to vote if you
   want to vote in the election.

3. It's illegal to loiter in front of the White House. People _____
   in front of the White House.

4. The sign says "No trespassing". That means we _____ the
   building.

5. There is no admission fee for children under the age of five. Children under the age of five
   _____ to get in.

6. The Constitution says that a law _____ constitutional. It cannot break the rules of the Constitution.

7. The Constitution says that the President signs a bill before it is law. The President
   _____ a bill before it becomes a law.

8. You can park for free here. You _____ to park here.

9. The plane cannot take off until all passengers are seated. You _____ now.

10. It is against the law to text while you are driving. You _____
    while texting.

Unit 9: Government

Major National Holidays

A Match each holiday to its description.

_____ 1. Martin Luther King, Jr. Day

_____ 2. Presidents' Day

_____ 3. Memorial Day

_____ 4. Independence Day

_____ 5. Labor Day

a. On this day, we celebrate workers. This holiday takes place on the first Monday in September.

b. This holiday occurs in the summer. It celebrates the day that the United States approved the Declaration of Independence.

c. This holiday takes place on the last Monday in May. It honors people who died while serving in the U.S. military.

d. On this day, we celebrate important U.S. politicians. This holiday takes place in February.

e. This holiday celebrates an important civil rights leader, and it occurs on the third Monday in January.

B Write the sentences from the box in the correct places in the conversation.

- That sounds like fun. I love the beach.
- Unfortunately, I have to study over the weekend.
- Oh, I'd love to, but I have other plans on Labor Day.
- That's right. And we have the day off.

A: Next Monday is Labor Day.

B: _____

_____

A: My friends and I are going to the beach.

B: _____

_____

A: You should come with us.

B: _____

_____

A: How about Saturday and Sunday? We're going to be at the beach all weekend.

B: _____

_____

C Read about George Washington and Abraham Lincoln. Then answer the questions. Use complete sentences.

Two Important U.S. Presidents

George Washington was born on February 22, 1732. On April 30, 1789, he became the first president of the United States. He stayed in office until March 4, 1797. Before he became president, he earned the trust and admiration of the American people as a general in the war against England. One of the most famous stories about Washington is not about his time as general or as president. The story is about Washington as a boy. One day, young George cut down a cherry tree. When his father asked him if he had cut the tree down, he was afraid that he would be punished if he told the truth. But he told the truth anyway, saying, "I cannot tell a lie."

Abraham Lincoln was born on February 12, 1809, to a poor family and lived in a log cabin, which is a small house made of tree trunks. Although his family didn't have any money, Lincoln worked hard to get an education. He read every book that he could find. Eventually, he became a lawyer, and then, the 16th president of the United States. He held office from March 4, 1861 to April 15, 1865. People often refer to Lincoln by his nickname, Honest Abe. No one is really sure how he got the nickname, but some people say that it is because one day, when he was working in a store as a young man, he gave someone the wrong change. When he realized what he had done, he followed the customer a long way to give him the rest of his change.

1. When was George Washington born?

   _____

2. What did Washington do during the war against England?

   _____

3. How long was Washington president of the United States?

   _____

4. When was Lincoln born?

   _____

5. How long was Lincoln president of the United States?

   _____

6. What do the two stories mentioned in the reading say about Washington and Lincoln?

   _____

7. Why do you think these stories are so famous?

   _____

Registering to Vote

A Read about the two propositions. Then answer the questions for each.

Proposition 14: Housing and Emergency Shelter Act

This proposition will provide clean and safe housing for abused women and homeless and low-income families. It will also provide money for repairs and improvements to existing emergency shelters. In addition, it will provide money for apartments with medical staff on-hand for disabled and mentally ill citizens.

Proposition 14 will cost the state about $4.2 billion. About 30% of the funds will come from state income taxes. The state will use public land, such as parks, to build new housing.

---

1. Would you vote *yes* or *no* on Proposition 14? _____

2. Why would you vote *yes* or *no*? Give two reasons.

_____

_____

_____

_____

Proposition 27: Textbook Purchase/Arts Education Act

Proposition 27 will require public school students from kindergarten to grade 12 to pay for their textbooks. Right now, students use textbooks for free. Under Proposition 27, children will own the textbooks that they buy. Schools will be permitted to purchase used textbooks and re-sell them to new students. Schools may also earn a 10% profit on any used textbook sold.

The money that schools currently spend on student textbooks will be given to arts education, such as music, drama, and fine arts classes.

---

1. Would you vote *yes* or *no* on Proposition 27? _____
2. Why would you vote *yes* or *no*? Give two reasons.

_____

_____

_____

_____

B Check the requirements for voting in a state election in the United States.

REQUIREMENT	CHECK (✓)
1. You are at least 21 years of age (or will be by the next election).	
2. You are a resident of the state.	
3. You speak English.	
4. You are a United States citizen.	
5. You have been a United States citizen for at least 2 years.	
6. You are not in prison.	
7. You have never been in prison.	
8. You have registered to vote at least 10 days before the election.	
9. You have a driver's license.	
10. You have a U.S. Permanent Resident Card.	

C Read the situations. Write advice for each person using *should, why don't, or why doesn't.*

1. I am upset about a new proposition that requires students in grades K-12 to pay for books.

   _____

2. My town has a water problem. The water is not clean, and the town is not doing anything to clean it up.

   _____

3. Cesar wants to vote, but he doesn't know where to go.

   _____

4. Leila just got a part-time job as a lab technician, but she doesn't get any health benefits. She thinks this is unfair.

   _____

5. Lynn has a job interview at 2:00. Her bus is stuck in traffic, and she thinks she is going to be late.

   _____

Reading: Using the Dictionary

A Read the dictionary entry and answer the questions.

> **proposition** /prɑpəˈzɪʃən/ *n* **1** an idea or opinion about something: *Do you accept the proposition that human beings are responsible for protecting the environment?* **2** an offer or a suggestion: *Mr. Kim called with an interesting business proposition.* **3** a suggestion for a change to existing state law: *Did you vote no on Proposition 4?*

1. What word is this dictionary entry for? _____

2. What part of speech is the word? _____

3. How many meanings are given? _____

4. Which is the correct meaning for the way the word is used in this sentence?

   *Should we accept the **proposition** to sell the company?*

   _____

5. Which is the correct meaning for the way the word is used in this sentence?

   *I'm not sure how I feel about **Proposition** 12.*

   _____

B Read the proposition. Look up the highlighted words in a dictionary. For each word, write the part of speech, the number of definitions given for the word, and the correct dictionary definition for the way the word is used in the description.

> **Proposition 33**
>
> **School Facilities Initiative**
>
> This proposition authorizes certain county education offices to issue bonds for construction, reconstruction, rehabilitation or replacement of school facilities. Bonds will be issued to county education offices that evaluate school safety, class size, and technology needs.
>
> County education offices will be subject to annual performance reviews.
>
> Bonds will not be used for salaries or other school operating expenses.

1. **facility:** Part of speech: _____ Number of definitions: _____

   Dictionary definition: _____

   _____

2. **issue:** Part of speech: _____ Number of definitions: _____

   Dictionary definition: _____

   _____

3. **evaluate:** Part of speech: _____ Number of definitions: _____

   Dictionary definition: _____

   _____

4. **review:** Part of speech: _____ Number of definitions: _____

   Dictionary definition: _____

   _____

C Read the sentences below. Write your guess for the definition of each underlined word. Then write the correct dictionary definition for the way the word is used.

1. The state will <u>impose</u> a fee on any business that pollutes the environment.

   Your guess: _____

   Dictionary definition: _____

2. The report <u>excluded</u> information about the company's past legal problems.

   Your guess: _____

   Dictionary definition: _____

3. The law does not <u>apply to</u> minors under the age of 18.

   Your guess: _____

   Dictionary definition: _____

4. The bill provides $2 billion to <u>relieve</u> overcrowding in public schools.

   Your guess: _____

   Dictionary definition: _____

Writing: Stating Your Position

A Read the letter and answer the questions.

The Honorable Tina Kim
House Office Building
United States House of Representatives
Washington, DC 20515

Dear Representative Kim:

This year, Congress will vote on a bill to provide $2 billion to protect rivers, lakes, streams, beaches, and coastal areas threatened by pollution. This bill will ensure the improvement of water quality and availability of clean drinking water. It will also ensure improvement of air quality in urban areas and the preservation of state neighborhoods and parks.

Clean air and water are necessary for quality of life, and we should do everything we can to ensure that our air and water are not polluted. Currently, the air in my town is full of smog and pollution. My family has to drink filtered or bottled water because our drinking water is full of chemicals. The air and water quality in my town was better ten years ago. If we don't do something to protect our environment, I'm afraid that the situation is only going to get worse.

I urge you to support this bill when it comes up for a vote later this year.

Sincerely,

Tomas Ruiz

1. Who is Tomas writing to? _____

2. What issue is he concerned about? _____
_____

3. What is Tomas's position on the issue? _____
_____

4. What are Tomas's supporting ideas? Where does he explain these ideas?
_____
_____

5. Where does Tomas tell the representative to do something? Underline the persuasion expression that he uses.
_____

B Think of an issue that you are concerned about. Complete the chart below.

Issue:
My position:
Supporting ideas:

C Write a letter to your local representative. Use the ideas in Activity B.

_____

_____

_____

_____

_____

_____

_____

_____

_____

_____

_____

_____

Sincerely,

_____

Family: Education

A Read the description of the U.S. educational system and circle the correct answer to each question.

In the United States, education is free for all students attending public school from kindergarten through grade 12. Elementary school includes kindergarten through fifth or sixth grade. In some states, the next level is called middle school, and it includes grades five or six through eighth grade. In other states, the next level is known as junior high school, and it includes grades 7 and 8 (and sometimes 9). Secondary school, or high school, consists of grades 9 through 12 or 10 through 12. After secondary school, students can go on to post-secondary education, which may be a two-year junior college or community college, or a four-year college or university.

Usually, students must pass a statewide test at the end of the school year in certain grades in order to progress to the next grade. In some states, students must pass an exam in order to graduate from high school. In other states, students may graduate with passing grades in their classes. Schools vary in the type of grading system they use. Some schools give grades as percentages, such as 80% or 95%. Other schools report student progress by a letter grade system. In the letter grade system, an A is the best, a B is very good, a C is average, and an F is a failure. In most schools, a D grade is not sufficient to pass to the next level.

> **Note:** *Grade* can mean the grade level a student is in (first, second, third, etc.) or the letter grade a student receives (A, B, C, D, F).

1. Michael is in third grade. What type of school does he probably attend?
   A. elementary   B. middle   c. high

2. What grade is not usually in a secondary school?
   A. 12   B. 10   c. 6

3. How many years does it take to complete junior college?
   A. 4   B. 6   c. 2

4. Which letter grade represents a failure?
   A. A   B. C   c. F

5. Look at the report card on the right. Which word best describes the student's performance?
   A. excellent   B. average to good   c. failing

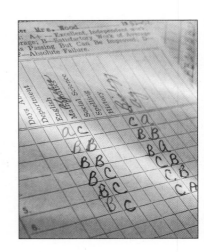

B Read the clues and look at the map below. Fill in the blanks with words from the box. Then match the questions and answers.

– The classrooms are in every building except the one with the library.
– There is only one classroom near the gym.
– The computer lab and the cafeteria are in the same building.
– The auditorium is not in Dickson.
– The student health clinic is next to the gym.

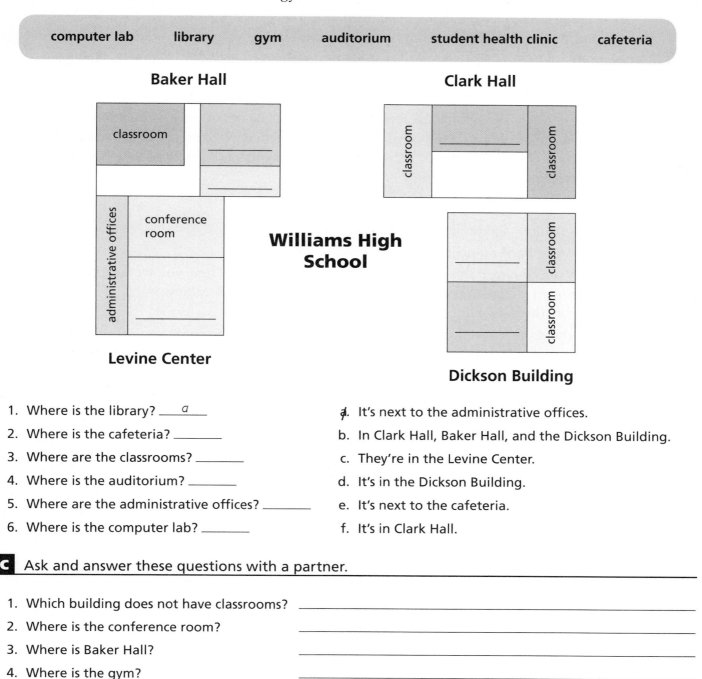

| computer lab | library | gym | auditorium | student health clinic | cafeteria |

Baker Hall

Clark Hall

classroom

Williams High School

conference room

administrative offices

Levine Center

Dickson Building

1. Where is the library? ___a___
2. Where is the cafeteria? _____
3. Where are the classrooms? _____
4. Where is the auditorium? _____
5. Where are the administrative offices? _____
6. Where is the computer lab? _____

a. It's next to the administrative offices.
b. In Clark Hall, Baker Hall, and the Dickson Building.
c. They're in the Levine Center.
d. It's in the Dickson Building.
e. It's next to the cafeteria.
f. It's in Clark Hall.

C Ask and answer these questions with a partner.

1. Which building does not have classrooms? _____
2. Where is the conference room? _____
3. Where is Baker Hall? _____
4. Where is the gym? _____

159

Work: Unemployment Insurance

A Read the information about unemployment insurance. Then read the statements and check *True* or *False*.

Filing for Unemployment

In the United States, if you are out of work or working less than full-time, you may be eligible to file a claim for unemployment insurance. This insurance is paid for by federal and state governments. If your claim is approved, you will receive a percentage of your most recent salary. You can usually file a claim online, by mail, over the telephone, or at your local state employment office. To find an office in your area, you can go to the U.S. Department of Labor's website and search for resources in your state.

In order to receive unemployment insurance, you must be out of work through no fault of your own. You must also be physically able to work, actively looking for work, and ready to work if a job is offered to you. When filing for unemployment, you will need to have the following information available:

- Your name and social security number
- Your mailing and residence addresses (if different)
- Your telephone number
- Your last employer information (regardless of the length of time you worked for the employer) including name, address (mailing and physical location) and telephone number (including area code)
- Information on all employers you worked for during the 18 months prior to submitting your applications and filing your claim, including name, period of employment, wages earned and how you were paid
- Your last date worked and the reason you are no longer working
- Your gross earnings in the last week you worked
- Your driver's license or ID card number, if you have either
- Your citizenship status (which may include your alien registration number)

	True	False
1. You can file for unemployment insurance online.	☐	☐
2. You can file for unemployment insurance at the U.S. Department of Labor.	☐	☐
3. Unemployment insurance money comes from both state and federal governments.	☐	☐
4. You may be eligible for unemployment insurance if you are injured and cannot work.	☐	☐
5. You must be trying to find a job to be eligible for unemployment insurance.	☐	☐

B Read the information about Mario. Then complete his unemployment insurance application.

Mario Jose Santos is filing for unemployment insurance. He was born on February 2, 1972 in Mexico City, Mexico. He graduated from high school in 1989, and he graduated from college with a Bachelor's Degree in Computer Science in 1993. His social security number is 955-00-2414.

He filed for unemployment insurance in California once before, five years ago. He is filing again now because he was laid off from his job. The company that he was working for, Mitchell Technologies, was losing money, so they laid off over 30 employees. The phone number at his last job is 415-555-9045. He worked there from July 1, 2009 to April 30, 2010. While he worked there, he earned $65,000. Before that, Mario worked at Lion Computer Systems. The phone number there is 408-555-3347. He had that job from January 15, 2007 to June 15, 2009. He earned $156,000 during that time.

1. What is your Social Security Number?	
2. What is your full name?	
3. What is your birth date?	(mo/day/yr)
4. What is your gender?	☐ Male ☐ Female
7. Have you filed an Unemployment Insurance claim in the last two years?	☐ Yes ☐ No

9. What is the highest grade of school you have completed? Check only one box.
☐ Did not complete High School ☐ High School Diploma or GED
☐ Some college or vocational school ☐ Associate of Arts
☐ Bachelor of Arts or Science ☐ Masters or Doctorate

Provide your employment and wages for the past 18 months.

a) Employer Name _____ b) Phone Number _____
c) Total Earnings _____ d) Dates Worked _____
e) Why did you leave? _____

a) Employer Name _____ b) Phone Number _____
c) Total Earnings _____ d) Dates Worked _____
e) Why did you leave? *got a new job*

Practice Test

DIRECTIONS: Read the letter below to answer the next 5 questions. Use the Answer Sheet.

The Honorable Alan Chow
House Office Building
United States House of Representatives
Washington, DC 20515

Dear Representative Chow:

Two years ago, Congress voted on a bill to provide children from low-income families with a free college education, and the President vetoed it. Next year, Congress will vote on this bill again. I believe that the government must provide a free college education to children who cannot otherwise afford to go to college.

A college education is very expensive. Even many middle-class parents have difficulty paying for their children's college tuitions. For most low-income parents, it's almost impossible to afford to send their children to four-year colleges. Many children have to work to go to college, and they can't focus on their studies. Children are the future leaders of this country, and we need to make sure they are prepared for the future.

I urge you to support free college education for children of low-income families when this bill is proposed again next year.

Sincerely,

Nicholas Tan

1. This letter is written to _____.
   A. a member of the senate
   B. a state governor
   C. a member of the House of Representatives
   D. the Speaker of the House

2. The writer is concerned about _____.
   A. free college education for everyone
   B. free college education for low-income children
   C. free public education for everyone
   D. free public education for low-income children

3. The writer wants Representative Chow to _____.
   A. vote for the bill
   B. vote against the bill
   C. propose the bill
   D. veto the bill

4. The president vetoed this bill _____.
   A. last year
   B. two years ago
   C. three years ago
   D. four years ago

5. The writer probably believes that _____.
   A. all children should have a college education
   B. all government leaders should have a college degree
   C. children should save their own money to go to college
   D. children should not work while they are in college

ANSWER SHEET

	A	B	C	D
1	A	B	C	D
2	A	B	C	D
3	A	B	C	D
4	A	B	C	D
5	A	B	C	D
6	A	B	C	D
7	A	B	C	D
8	A	B	C	D
9	A	B	C	D
10	A	B	C	D

DIRECTIONS: Read the information below to answer the next 5 questions. Use the Answer Sheet on page 162.

The state elections are tomorrow, November 2.

1. Anne is a U.S. citizen. She was just put in prison last week. She registered to vote three weeks ago.

2. Peter is a resident of Florida. He registered to vote in Florida a year ago. He got out of prison five years ago. He used to live in California. He will be in California during the election for state governor, and he wants to vote.

3. Ming is a U.S. citizen. She is 75 years old. She registered to vote a week ago. She doesn't speak English.

4. Margaret is a university student. She is a resident of Texas and has a permanent resident card. She is a citizen of China.

5. Alan is a U.S. citizen. He will turn 18 on December 15. He wants to vote in the November 2nd election. He speaks English.

6. Anne can't vote because _____.
   A. she registered too late
   B. she is not a U.S. citizen
   C. she is in prison
   D. she is too young

7. Peter can't vote because _____.
   A. he was in prison
   B. he registered too late
   C. he is not a resident of Florida
   D. he is not a resident of California

8. Ming can't vote because _____.
   A. she is too old
   B. she registered too late
   C. she doesn't speak English
   D. she is not registered

9. Margaret can't vote because _____.
   A. she doesn't have a permanent resident card
   B. she is still a student
   C. she is not a U.S. citizen
   D. she is too young

10. Alan can't vote because _____.
   A. he turns 18 after the election
   B. he is not a U.S. citizen
   C. he is not a resident of the state
   D. he registered too late

Identifying Jobs and Equipment

A Write the correct word from the box under each photo.

| air traffic controller | baggage handler | gate agent |
| ticket agent | airport security screener | aircraft maintenance technician |

1. _____

_____

2. _____

_____

3. _____

_____

4. _____

_____

5. _____

_____

6. _____

_____

B Write the correct word from the box under each photo.

x-ray scanner	boarding pass	tow tractor
metal detector	baggage	headset

1. _____

2. _____

3. _____

4. _____

5. _____

6. _____

C Complete the sentences with the correct reflexive pronoun.

1. The baggage handlers load the bags onto the plane by _____.

2. An airplane cannot back _____ up, so it has to be towed to the runway.

3. We're proud of _____ for finishing the job on time.

4. Julie likes her job because her boss lets her work by _____.

5. I fixed the DVD player _____.

6. The ticket agent cannot handle all the customers _____. He needs help.

7. You should give _____ a break after the next semester of school.

8. Juan called _____ to be sure his phone was working.

Understanding Work Schedules

A Read the sentences. Then write the missing information in the schedule.

1. Sarah is going to be on vacation from August 10 to August 19.
2. Lily has a doctor's appointment on August 16 at 1:00.
3. Peter has to take military leave from August 3 to January 3.
4. Raymond is taking a leave of absence from August 18 to October 1.
5. Jose has jury duty from August 22 to the end of that week.
6. Yoshiko has maternity leave from August 23 until November 23.

SHOPMART • LEAVE SCHEDULE • AUGUST

Monday	Tuesday	Wednesday	Thursday	Friday
Kate: **childcare emergency leave** to 8/5 **1**	**2**	Peter: **military leave** to _____ **3**	Ling: **bereavement leave** to 8/9 **4**	**5**
Marcus: dentist appt., 10:30 A.M. **8**	Ronaldo: **paternity leave** to 8/23 **9**	_____ : **vacation** to 8/19 **10**	**11**	Lucia: **medical leave** to 9/15 **12**
15	Lily: _____ _____ ,1 P.M. **16**	**17**	_____ : **leave of absence** to 10/1 **18**	**19**
Jose: **jury duty** to _____ **22**	Yoshiko: _____ _____ to 11/23 **23**	**24**	**25**	**26**

B Match each person from Activity A with the reason they are taking time off.

_____ 1. Kate   a. to have a baby and or take care of a new baby

_____ 2. Peter   b. to serve on a jury

_____ 3. Ling   c. to take care of children when there's no one to help

_____ 4. Marcus   d. to take a trip, rest, or spend time with others

_____ 5. Ronaldo   e. to serve in the military

_____ 6. Sarah   f. to do something other than work, for example, go to school

_____ 7. Lucia   g. for a serious medical reason, such as surgery

_____ 8. Lily   h. to see a dentist

_____ 9. Raymond   i. to see a doctor

_____ 10. Jose   j. because someone died

C Complete the sentences with your own ideas.

1. Sandra is taking a week of vacation because _____

_____

2. Marek asked his boss for time off since _____

_____

3. Because I have jury duty next week, _____

_____

4. Amir is on medical leave this month because _____

_____

5. My boss didn't give me time off since _____

_____

6. We weren't allowed to carry the bag on the plane because _____

_____

D Answer the questions with a complete sentence. Use *because* or *since*.

1. Why do people take bereavement leave?

_____

_____

2. Why do companies give their employees vacation time?

_____

_____

3. Why do managers keep a work schedule?

_____

_____

Leaving Phone Messages

A Are these phrases formal or informal? Write each phrase in the correct place in the chart.

Mr. Lee isn't in.	May I take a message?	Can I take a message?
Jack isn't here right now.	Do you want to leave a message?	She's not here.
Tina can't come to the phone right now.	Would you like to leave a message?	

Formal	Informal

B Complete the conversations below with your own ideas.

1. A: Ms. Wong's office.

    B: Hello. This is Rick Cooper. May I please speak to Ms. Wong?

    A: _____. May I take a message?

    B: Yes, would you please ask her to call me back? My number is 555-9033.

    A: _____.

    B: Thank you.

2. A: Hello.

    B: Hi. This is Kurt. Is Scott there?

    A: He isn't here right now. _____?

    B: Okay. Will you please tell him _____?

    A: Sure, I'll tell him.

3. A: Hello.

    B: Hi, Mia. This is Dan. Can I talk to Eric?

    A: Sorry, Dan. _____.

    _____?

    B: Sure. Can you tell him _____?

    A: No problem.

C Complete the chart with information from Activity B.

Who called?	Phone Number	Message
1.		
2.		
3.		

D Complete the sentences with the present perfect continuous. Use a verb that fits the sentence. Use contractions or full forms.

1. Get off the phone! You _____ for over two hours!

2. When are we going to get there? We _____ since 6:00 this morning and I'm tired.

3. My car broke down last week, so I _____ to school this week.

4. Oliva is still in the boss' office. They _____ the new project all morning.

5. My parents moved to La Grange in 1965, and we _____ ever since.

6. Please answer the phone. It _____ for five minutes.

7. Captain Richards is one of our best pilots. He _____ for 20 years.

8. This line isn't moving. How long _____ we _____ here?

9. Ray _____ for a promotion for two years and he finally got one today.

10. The children _____ for hours. They must be tired.

11. Angie _____ that book all day. It must be good.

12. I _____ money for two years and now I can buy a house.

Understanding W-2 Forms

A Look at the sample W-2 form. Check *True* or *False* for each statement.

a Control number 12378945	22222	Void ☐	For Official Use Only ▶ OMB No. 1545-0008	

b Employer identification number 00-9X45123		1 Wages, tips, other compensation 42,300	2 Federal income tax withheld 5,076.00
c Employer's name, address, and ZIP code Samson Computers 89314 18th Street San Francisco, CA 94114		3 Social security wages 42,300	4 Social security tax withheld 1,742.00
		5 Medicare wages and tips	6 Medicare tax withheld
		7 Social security tips	8 Allocated tips
d Employee's social security number 000-13-4564		9 Advance EIC payment	10 Dependent care benefits
e Employee's first name and initial Pedro M	Last name Reyes	11 Nonqualified plans	12a See instructions for box 12
1124 Maple Street, Apt.2 San Jose, CA 95101	13 Statutory employee ☐ Retirement plan ☐ Third-party sick pay ☐	12b
		14 Other	12c
			12d
f Employee's address and ZIP code			

15 State CA	Employer's state ID number XXX-XXX-XXX	16 State wages, tips, etc. 42,300	17 State income tax 2,027.00	18 Local wages, tips, etc.	19 Local income tax	20 Locality name

Form **W-2** Wage and Tax Statement   **2011**   Department of the Treasury—Internal Revenue Service

Copy A For Social Security Administration — Send this entire page with Form W-3 to the Social Security Administration; photocopies are **not** acceptable.

For Privacy Act and Paperwork Reduction Act Notice, see back of Copy D.

Cat. No. 10134D

Do Not Cut, Fold, or Staple Forms on This Page — Do Not Cut, Fold, or Staple Forms on This Page

	True	False
1. The employee's name is Pedro Reyes.	☐	☐
2. The employee works at 1124 Maple Street in San Jose.	☐	☐
3. He works for a computer company.	☐	☐
4. He earned $42,300 in 2011.	☐	☐
5. $5,076.00 was withheld for federal income tax.	☐	☐
6. $1,742.00 was withheld for state income tax.	☐	☐
7. $2,027.00 was withheld for social security tax.	☐	☐
8. The employee's social security number is 000-13-4564.	☐	☐

B Use the information in the W-2 form in Activity A to complete the form.

U.S. Individual Income Tax Return	2011	
Your first name and initial _____	Last Name _____	Your social security number _____ / ___ / _____
Home address (number and street) _____ _____		Apt. no. _____
City, town or post office, state, and ZIP code. _____		
1. Wages, salaries, tips, etc.		_____
2. Federal income tax		$5,458.00
3. Federal income tax withheld from Forms W-2 and 1099		$5,076.00
4. If the amount on line 3 is more than the amount on line 2, subtract line 2 from line 3. This is the amount you **overpaid**.		_____
5. If the amount on line 2 is more than the amount on line 3, subtract line 3 from line 2. This is the amount you owe.		_____
Sign here Your signature ___*Pedro Reyes*___		Date ___2/15/2012___

Reading: Pronoun Reference

A Read the article. Write the word or words that each boldface pronoun refers to.

How to Improve Your Interpersonal Skills

It's important to be responsible and do a good job at work, but interpersonal skills are just as important. Being able to get along with the people that you work with is a crucial workplace skill. If your boss and coworkers don't enjoy working with you, you may not get the raises and promotions you feel you deserve. If your interpersonal skills need some work, here are six things you can do to improve **them**.

1. Pay attention to your coworkers and listen to **their** ideas. Don't just wait for **them** to stop talking and then start giving your own opinion or your own story. Restate their opinions and comment on their ideas to show that you understand **them**. Make sure to use body language that shows you are listening. For example, don't tap your fingers on the table or look around while people are talking to you. **They** will think you aren't paying attention. Instead, look at people when they are talking to you.

2. Pay attention to your own communication. What do you sound like when you share ideas or opinions at work? Do you sound angry? Disrespectful? Be aware of the things you say and how you say **them**.

3. Don't complain about work or your personal life to your boss and coworkers. Of course, if you have a serious problem at work, you should talk about **it** with your boss. But don't become known as the person who complains all the time.

4. Get to know your coworkers during lunch breaks and relaxed moments at work. If you are shy and have trouble thinking of things to say to people, ask them questions. For example, you can ask a coworker what he's doing over the weekend or find out what kinds of things **he** likes to do for fun.

5. If you walk past your coworkers with a frown on your face, and you don't look at them, they may think that you're being rude. Smile at people and be friendly. A cheerful attitude attracts people. **It** also helps people feel relaxed around you.

6. Appreciate the things that other people contribute to your workplace. If a coworker does something nice for you or something that makes your job easier, thank **her** for it.

1. them _____

2. their _____

3. them _____

4. them _____

5. They _____

6. them _____

7. it _____

8. he _____

9. It _____

10. her _____

B Answer the questions about the article.

1. What should you *not* do when someone is telling you an idea, an opinion, or a story?

   _____

2. How can you show people that you are paying attention to what they are saying?

   _____

3. How can it help to smile and be cheerful at work?

   _____

4. What can you do if you're shy and have trouble thinking of things to say to people?

   _____

5. Why are interpersonal skills important?

   _____

6. What can you do to improve your own interpersonal skills?

   _____

C Read each pair of sentences. Write the word or phrase that the boldface pronoun refers to.

Sentences	What the pronoun refers to
1. Mike won't be here next week. **He** is taking bereavement leave.	_____
2. I'm taking a vacation next month. **It's** going to be so much fun!	_____
3. Joe has jury duty at the county courthouse, not the federal courthouse. **It's** the one on 3rd Street.	_____
4. Lee took a leave of absence to take a management course. He's taking **it** at the community college.	_____
5. Mary is on maternity leave, but she brought her new baby into work yesterday. She let me hold **her** for a while.	_____
6. Jack and Lily are both taking their vacations this month. **They'll** be back next Friday.	_____

Writing: Writing Professional Emails

A Check *True* or *False* for each statement.

	True	False
1. You should include a clear subject line in professional emails.	☐	☐
2. You should use all capital letters when you want to emphasize an idea.	☐	☐
3. It's okay to discuss private information in professional emails because business emails are confidential.	☐	☐
4. You don't have to include your name in a closing at the end of a professional email because your name is in your email address.	☐	☐
5. You should keep professional emails as short as possible and stay on topic.	☐	☐

B Read the email below. Underline the mistakes that the writer made. There are three types of mistakes. Write the types of mistakes below the email.

From: PSimpson@spd.com

Subject: Request for Leave of Absence

Date: March 14, 2010
To: SJones@spd.com

Dear Ms. Jones:

I am emailing you to request a three-month leave of absence. I'd like to take September 19 to December 19 off to go back to school. I need one more semester to get my Bachelor's Degree. I started college in 1996, but I wasn't able to continue after my daughter was born. Now that she's a teenager, I can go back. I WANT TO GET MY DEGREE BEFORE SHE GETS HERS!

Also, I'm hoping that I can make a higher salary once I have my college degree. I know that some of my coworkers who have college degrees make more money than I do. Mark told me that he earns $5,000 more a year than his boss does because he has a degree.

Please let me know if you have any questions, and if my leave of absence is approved.

Thank you.

Pam Simpson

The mistakes:

1. _____

2. _____

3. _____

C Ask for time off for a vacation or a leave of absence. Think of the amount of time that you need to take off from work and a brief explanation for your request. Complete the chart.

Type of leave:
_____
Time you need to take off:
_____
Explanation:
_____
_____
_____
_____
_____

D Write an email to Ms. Jones (SJones@spd.com). Ask for time off from work. Use the ideas in your chart from Activity C.

FROM: _____

SUBJECT: _____

DATE: _____

TO: _____

_____:

_____

_____

_____

_____

_____

_____

_____

_____

_____

Work: Job Interviews

A Read the information about job interviews.

How to Make a Good Impression at a Job Interview

Before the interview, make sure you know exactly where and when the interview will be. Plan to arrive at least 10 minutes early. You may want to go to the location ahead of time to make sure you know how long it will take to get there. Dress appropriately for the type of job environment; that means a suit for a business environment, and clean and neat attire for any position. Most of all, prepare for the interview by anticipating questions and composing answers. Think of a few intelligent questions to ask the interviewer. If possible, research some basic information about the company on the Internet.

accomplishments	things you have done or learned well
anticipating	thinking of something before it happens
attire	clothing
composing	writing
environment	the things and conditions that are in and around a place
eye contact	the act of looking directly into someone else's eyes
impression	a lasting belief or opinion

During the interview, maintain good posture. Sit up in your chair, look attentive, and maintain good eye contact throughout the interview. Shake hands firmly and speak in a clear, confident voice. Take the interview seriously, be polite, and demonstrate a positive attitude. Don't chew gum or smoke. Your cell phone should be turned off.

When answering questions, use the interviewer's title and last name (such as Ms. Smith, Mr. Johnson). Answer questions completely, but don't go on too long. Give specific examples when possible. Be honest. If you are not wonderful at something, acknowledge that it is something you are trying to improve. Talk about your accomplishments and experience. Demonstrate that you know something about the company or organization and ask intelligent questions.

After the interview, write notes about the experience for your own records. You will want to remember people's names and other specific information when you speak to them again. Write a thank-you letter to the interviewer within a few days.

B Circle the things you should do in an interview. Use information from Activity A.

answer questions at length	ask questions	chew gum
shake hands with female interviewers	smoke	speak softly
talk on your cell phone	tell the truth	wear jeans
call the office a day after the interview	sit comfortably	make jokes
avoid your interviewer's eyes	write notes after the interview	arrive early

C Match the statement with the tip.

_____ 1. "Nice to meet you, Ms. Hunter."

_____ 2. "I'm very proud of the award I received two years ago for outstanding performance."

_____ 3. "I understand the company is growing rapidly. Do you plan to open other offices?"

_____ 4. "Ideally, I'd like to be in a management position in the next five years."

_____ 5. "I think our strengths are also sometimes our weaknesses. My willingness to share ideas is a good thing, but I'm trying to make sure that I don't keep other people from sharing their ideas."

a. Be honest about your weaknesses.

b. Ask intelligent questions to show you know something about the company.

c. Share accomplishments.

d. Talk about career goals.

e. Be polite and respectful.

D Read the interviewer's comments and questions. Then write the responses from Activity C on the lines. Practice the conversation with a partner.

Interviewer: Good morning, Adam. I'm Gwen Hunter. It's nice to meet you.

Adam: _____

Interviewer: I see that you've worked in this field before.

Adam: Yes, I have eight years of experience in commercial real estate.

Interviewer: What are the strengths you bring to this position?

Adam: I'm very good with clients and very responsible.

Interviewer: What weaknesses do you think you have?

Adam: _____

_____

_____

Interviewer: And what do you think has been your greatest accomplishment so far?

Adam: _____

_____

Interviewer: Where do you see yourself in the next five or ten years?

Adam: _____

_____

Interviewer: Do you have any questions for me?

Adam: _____

_____

Community: The Department of Labor

A Read the information. Then, check *True* or *False* for each statement.

The U.S. Department of Labor is a Cabinet department of the U.S. Government. Its office is in Washington D.C. The head of this department is the Secretary of Labor, who is chosen by the President and then must be approved by the Senate. The Department of Labor is responsible for safety, fair wages, hour standards, unemployment insurance benefits, rights, and employment services of workers in the United States. It is also responsible for calculating statistics relating to labor, such as the number of people in the United States who are unemployed at a particular time.

The Department of Labor provides many services to workers. For example, it pays for training programs throughout the country. Most of the training programs can be found through the One-Stop Career Center system. You can access this system online at http://www.servicelocator.org/ or by telephone at 1-877-US2JOBS (1-877-872-5627).

The Department of Labor also protects workers against discrimination in the workplace. Anyone who believes they were fired, mistreated, or not hired because of their race, religion, age, disability, political beliefs, or any other personal reason can turn to the DoL for assistance.

In addition, the Department of Labor provides job and training information for people who may have difficulty finding jobs or receiving training. For example, disabled workers, senior citizens, military veterans, and people who have been laid off or will soon be laid off from their jobs can benefit from the Department of Labor.

	True	False
1. The head of the Department of Labor is the President of the United States.	☐	☐
2. In order to become Secretary of Labor, a candidate must be approved by the Senate.	☐	☐
3. The Department of Labor keeps track of the number of people in the United States who are unemployed.	☐	☐
4. If you are fired from your job because of a disability, the Department of Labor can give you a job.	☐	☐
5. The Department of Labor provides most of its training programs at its office in Washington D.C.	☐	☐
6. If you have been laid off from your job, you can get information about training programs through the Department of Labor.	☐	☐

B Read the information and answer the questions.

Frequently Asked Questions (FAQs)

Question: I am a single mother with no work skills. Where can I go for help?

Answer: We suggest you contact Women Work! The National Network for Women's Employment head-quartered in Washington, D.C. They assist women with career counseling, job placement, job readiness, and life skills development, and have offices throughout the country. To find the office closest to you, call 202-467-6346.

Question: I just found out that I am pregnant. Can my employer fire me or reassign me?

Answer: No. Under the Civil Rights Act of 1964 an employer with 15 or more employees can not fire you because you are pregnant, and must permit you to continue working as long as you are able. Some states have laws that cover employers with less than 15 employees. If you work for an employer with less than 15 employees, check with your regional Women's Bureau Office to see if your state has an agency that can assist you.

Question: What hours can youth work?

Answer: Under the Fair Labor Standards Act (FLSA), the minimum age for employment in non-agricultural employment is 14. Hours worked by most 14- and 15-year-olds are limited to:

- Non-school hours;
- 3 hours in a school day;
- 18 hours in a school week;
- 8 hours on a non-school day;
- 40 hours on a non-school week; and
- hours between 7 A.M. and 7 P.M. (except from June 1 through Labor Day, when evening hours are extended to 9 P.M.)

1. What number can you call for help finding a job if you are a single mother with no work skills?

   _____

2. What services are provided by the organization Women Work! The National Network for Women's Employment?

   _____

3. If you are fired because you are pregnant, and your employer has fewer than 15 employees, where can you go for help?

   _____

4. How many hours can a 14-year-old work on a school day and in a school week?

   _____

Practice Test

DIRECTIONS: Read the schedule to answer the next 5 questions. Use the Answer Sheet.

FEBRUARY

Monday	Tuesday	Wednesday	Thursday	Friday
Ana: **military leave** to 4/17 **3**	**4**	Tina: **medical leave** to 3/1 **5**	**6**	Pedro: **bereavement leave** to 2/11 **7**
Ruby: **jury duty** to 2/14 **10**	Ming: **childcare emergency leave** to 2/18 **11**	Luis: **paternity leave** to 3/4 **12**	Sandra: **maternity leave** to 5/5 **13**	Ed: **leave of absence** to 4/15 **14**

1. Ana is going to be away from work for _____.
   A. two weeks
   B. about one and a half months
   C. about two and a half months
   D. about three months

2. Pedro is taking leave because _____.
   A. he has a medical problem
   B. he has to have surgery
   C. he has to take care of his child
   D. someone he knows has died

3. Ruby has to take time off _____.
   A. because she was arrested
   B. to help make a decision in a court of law
   C. because she is a lawyer
   D. to learn about how the court system works

4. Tina probably _____.
   A. is going to have surgery
   B. has to take care of her son after he has surgery
   C. wants to go back to school
   D. has a bad cold

5. Luis is taking time off _____.
   A. to go on vacation
   B. to help take care of his new baby
   C. to go back to school
   D. to take care of his sick child

ANSWER SHEET

1 Ⓐ Ⓑ Ⓒ Ⓓ
2 Ⓐ Ⓑ Ⓒ Ⓓ
3 Ⓐ Ⓑ Ⓒ Ⓓ
4 Ⓐ Ⓑ Ⓒ Ⓓ
5 Ⓐ Ⓑ Ⓒ Ⓓ
6 Ⓐ Ⓑ Ⓒ Ⓓ
7 Ⓐ Ⓑ Ⓒ Ⓓ
8 Ⓐ Ⓑ Ⓒ Ⓓ
9 Ⓐ Ⓑ Ⓒ Ⓓ
10 Ⓐ Ⓑ Ⓒ Ⓓ

DIRECTIONS: Read the W-2 form to answer the next 5 questions. Use the Answer Sheet on page 180.

a Control number 12378945	22222	Void ☐	For Official Use Only ▶ OMB No. 1545-0008		
b Employer identification number 00-88X9076			1 Wages, tips, other compensation 35,200		2 Federal income tax withheld 2,806.00
c Employer's name, address, and ZIP code Cafe Rose 2215 Jones Street Miami, FL 33122			3 Social security wages 35,200		4 Social security tax withheld 1,154.00
			5 Medicare wages and tips 35,200		6 Medicare tax withheld 372.00
			7 Social security tips		8 Allocated tips
d Employee's social security number 000-14-2131			9 Advance EIC payment		10 Dependent care benefits
e Employee's first name and initial Elisa	Last name Chu		11 Nonqualified plans		12a See instructions for box 12
892 8th Ave Miami, FL 33137			13 Statutory employee ☐ Retirement plan ☐ Third-party sick pay ☐		12b
			14 Other		12c
					12d
f Employee's address and ZIP code					

15 State CA	Employer's state ID number XXX-XXX-XXX	16 State wages, tips, etc. 35,200	17 State income tax 1,683.00	18 Local wages, tips, etc.	19 Local income tax	20 Locality name

Form **W-2** Wage and Tax Statement **2011** Department of the Treasury—Internal Revenue Service

Copy A For Social Security Administration — Send this entire page with Form W-3 to the Social Security Administration; photocopies are **not** acceptable.

For Privacy Act and Paperwork Reduction Act Notice, see back of Copy D.

Cat. No. 10134D

Do Not Cut, Fold, or Staple Forms on This Page — Do Not Cut, Fold, or Staple Forms on This Page

6. Elisa Chu earned _____ in 2011.
   A. $35,200.00
   B. $32,500.00
   C. $23,5.00
   D. $35,020.00

7. $2,806.00 was withheld for _____.
   A. Social security tax
   B. Local income tax
   C. Medicare tax
   D. Federal income tax

8. $1,683.00 was withheld for _____.
   A. State income tax
   B. Local income tax
   C. Social security tax
   D. Federal income tax

9. The smallest amount withheld was for _____.
   A. State income tax
   B. Social security tax
   C. Medicare tax
   D. Federal income tax

10. The largest amount withheld was for _____.
   A. State income tax
   B. Social security tax
   C. Local income tax
   D. Federal income tax

All-Star Student Book 3 / All-Star Workbook 3

Correlation Table

Student Book Pages	Workbook Pages	Student Book Pages	Workbook Pages
PRE-UNIT		**UNIT 4**	
2–3		46–47	56–57
		48–49	58–59
UNIT 1		50–51	60–61
4–5	2–3	52–53	62–63, 68–71
6–7	4–5	54–55	64–65
8–9	6–7	56–57	66–67
10–11	8–9, 14–17	58–59	72–73
12–13	10–11		
14–15	12–13	**UNIT 5**	
16–17	18–19	60–61	74–75
		62–63	76–77
UNIT 2		64–65	78–79
18–19	20–21	66–67	80–81, 86–89
20–21	22–23	68–69	82–83
22–23	24–25	70–71	84–85
24–25	26–27, 32–35	72–73	90–91
26–27	28–29		
28–29	30–31	**UNIT 6**	
30–31	36–37	74–75	92–93
		76–77	94–95
UNIT 3		78–79	96–97
32–33	38–39	80–81	98–99, 104–107
34–35	40–41	82–83	100–101
36–37	42–43	84–85	102–103
38–39	44–45, 50–53	86–87	108–109
40–41	46–47		
42–43	48–49		
44–45	54–55		

Student Book Pages	Workbook Pages	Student Book Pages	Workbook Pages
UNIT 7		UNIT 9	
88–89	110–111	116–117	146–147
90–91	112–113	118–119	148–149
92–93	114–115	120–121	150–151
94–95	116–117, 122–125	122–123	152–153, 158–161
96–97	118–119	124–125	154–155
98–99	120–121	126–127	156–157
100–101	126–127	128–129	162–163
UNIT 8		UNIT 10	
102–103	128–129	130–131	164–165
104–105	130–131	132–133	166–167
106–107	132–133	134–135	168–169
108–109	134–135, 140–143	136–137	170–171, 176–179
110–111	136–137	138–139	172–173
112–113	138–139	140–141	174–175
114–115	144–145	142–143	180–181

Credits

All multiple photos on page, credits read left to right on page or top to bottom in a column.

Page 2: Photodisc/Getty; **4:** The McGraw-Hill Companies, Gary He; Monica Lau/Getty; **6:** DigitalVision; **8:** S. Meltzer/Photolink/Getty; **10:** Blend Images/Getty; **15:** Image 100, Ltd.; **20:** BrandX Pictures; Ryan McVay/Getty; **22:** Rubberball Productions; 2009 JupiterImages; **23:** Imagestate Media/John Foxx; BananaStock/age footstock; **24:** Ryan McVay/Getty; **25:** Ingram Publishing/Superstock; Janis Christie/Getty; **32:** Jules Frazia/Getty; Stockbyte/Getty; **39:** Ameil Skelley/Getty; RF/Corbis; Ryan McVay/Getty; **40:** Stockbyte/Punchstock; **42:** Ingram Publishing/AGE footstock; **44:** RF/Corbis; Photodisc/Getty; **46:** Ryan McVay/Getty; **48:** Bananastock/footstock; **50:** Ryan McVay/Getty; **51:** Thomas Northcut/Getty; **52:** Comstock/Alamy; Ryan McVay/Getty; Thinkstock Images/JupiterImages; **56:** Photodisc/Getty; Ryan McVay/Getty; **57:** Ryan McVay/Getty; Ingram Publishing/footstock; **58:** RF/Corbis; **60:** Skip Nall/Getty; **63:** BrandX/Photostock; **64:** RF/Corbis; David Buffington/Getty; Hisham F. Ibrahim/Getty; **65:** Comstock; Nicola Sutton/Life Files/Getty; **71:** Adam Crowley/Getty, **72:** PhotoAlto; **74:** Ingram Publishing/Alamy; **76:** Jack Star/Photolink/Getty; Stockbyte; Jack Star/Photolink/Getty; Ryan McVay/Getty; Nick Koudis/Getty; **78:** RF/Getty; **79:** Image Source; **81:** Nancy R. Cohen/Getty; Barbara Penoyar/Getty; RF/Corbis; **83:** RF/Corbis; **84:** RF/Corbis; RF/Corbis; **86:** The McGraw-Hill Companies, Ken Karp; **94:** RF/Corbis; Jules Frazier/Getty; Alamy Images; RF/Corbis; Tracey Hebden/Alamy; **95:** S. Solum/Photolink/Getty; Kent Knudson/Photolink/Getty; Nova Development; James Hardy/Photo Alto; **98:** BananaStock/Punchstock; RF/Corbis; Dex Image/Getty; **100:** Jack Star/Photolink/Getty; **101:** Emily A. White; S. Meltzer/Photolink/Getty; **104:** Hisham F. Ibrahim/Getty; **106:** Stockbyte/Getty; **109:** C. Squared Studios/Getty; **111:** RF/Corbis; RF/Corbis; Adam Crowley/Getty; Colorblend Images/age footstock; RF/Corbis; Corbis; **112:** The McGraw-Hill Companies, Lars Niki; **113:** Jack Hollingsworth/Corbis; **114:** Ryan McVay/Corbis; **116:** Adam Crowley/Getty; **118:** RF/Corbis; **123:** Stockdisc/Punchstock; **125:** BrandX Pictures/Punchstock; **128:** RF/Corbis; Barbara Penoyer/Getty; RF/Corbis; DigitalVision/Getty; Steve Cole/Getty; RF/Corbis; **132:** Stockbyte/Punchstock; **134:** Big Cheese Photo/JupiterImages; **137:** Ariel Skelley/age footstock; Andrew Wakefield/Getty; RF/Corbis; Photodisc/Getty; **140:** ImageSource/PictureQuest; **141:** Bananastock/PictureQuest; **158:** RF/Corbis; **164:** Corbis Premium/Alamy; ImageBank; Creatas/Punchstock; Getty; DigitalVision/Getty; Getty; **165:** Getty; Erik Isakson; ImageBank.